Goose berry Patch Co. ®

A Country Store In Your Mailbox ®

# Gifts for giving

best wishes

for you ♥

Caramel Sauce

*A Country Store In Your Mailbox*®

Gooseberry Patch
600 London Road
Department Book
Delaware, OH 43015
★
1·800·854·6673
gooseberrypatch.com

How To Subscribe

Would you like to receive
"A Country Store in Your Mailbox"®?
For a 2-year subscription to our 96-page
**Gooseberry Patch** catalog, simply send $3.00 to:

Gooseberry Patch
600 London Road
Delaware, OH 43015

Stock up on paper-edger scissors & punches.

Tie a set of measuring spoons to a cookbook... clever gift!

Super special gifts

Vintage rick-rack

# Contents

spread JOY!

Have a rubber stamp made with your initial~ stamp it on totes, flour sack towels, you name it!

Visit flea markets & gather up an armload of collanders & flour sifters.

Whoever is Happy will make others happy too.
— Anne Frank

# Dedication

To all of you who love to give handmade gifts from the heart to friends & family on holidays, birthdays and anytime!

Tear a raggedy strip of homespun & sew the ends to a paper bag (as shown) for a fun little tote.

Set a yummy mix inside a new cookie jar to welcome a new neighbor.

Fill the pocket of an apron with a cookie mix.

# cookies

Tie on a cookie cutter and a bag of sprinkles.

Fill a sparkly party hat with festive birthday cookies.

Decorate cookies like ornaments and give in a vintage ornament box.

Stack cookies inside an oatmeal or potato chip canister.

# Red, White & Chocolate Cookie Mix

*White chocolate and cherries combine for picnic-perfect flavor!*

3/4 c. all-purpose flour
1/4 t. baking soda
1/8 t. salt
1/4 c. baking cocoa
1/4 c. sugar

1/4 c. brown sugar, packed
1/4 c. white chocolate chips
1/3 c. dried cherries, chopped
1/3 c. chopped walnuts

Combine flour, baking soda and salt; place into a one-pint, wide-mouth jar. Layer remaining ingredients in order listed, firmly packing after each addition. Secure lid; attach gift tag with baking instructions.

## Instructions:

Remove walnuts, dried cherries and white chocolate chips from jar; place in a small bowl and toss to combine. In a separate bowl, cream 1/3 cup butter; blend in dry ingredients from jar. Beat in one egg and 1/2 teaspoon cherry extract. Gently stir in walnuts, dried cherries and white chocolate chips. Drop by level tablespoons onto a lightly greased baking sheet. Bake at 325 degrees for 14 to 16 minutes. Makes 1-1/2 dozen.

Hooray for the USA! Pair this mix with a box of sparklers and a couple of mini flags to light up 4th of July celebrations.

# Cookies

## Chocolatey Shortbread

*A yummy twist on an old-fashioned favorite!*

1 c. butter, softened
1-1/2 c. powdered sugar
1 egg
1 t. vanilla extract

2 c. all-purpose flour
1/2 c. baking cocoa
1/4 t. salt

Cream butter and sugar until fluffy; add egg and vanilla, beating until smooth. In a separate bowl, combine flour, cocoa and salt; add to creamed mixture. Stir until a soft dough forms; divide dough in half. Wrap in plastic wrap and chill for one hour. On a lightly floured surface, roll dough to 1/4-inch thickness. Use cookie cutters to cut out desired shapes; place on ungreased baking sheets. Bake at 375 degrees for 5 to 7 minutes. Move cookies to a wire rack to cool. Makes 4 dozen.

Surprise friends with a homemade cookie wreath...just arrange cut-out cookies in a heart shape before baking and be sure the sides overlap. Bake as usual and enjoy!

# Butterscotch-Oat Drop Cookies

*So easy to whip up for potlucks & carry-ins.*

6-oz. pkg. butterscotch chips
3/4 c. margarine
1 t. baking soda
2 T. boiling water
1/2 c. sugar

1 c. all-purpose flour
1/4 t. salt
2 c. quick-cooking oats,
    uncooked

Melt butterscotch chips and margarine together in a double boiler; remove from heat. Dissolve baking soda in boiling water; add to butterscotch mix. Gradually blend in remaining ingredients. Drop by rounded teaspoonfuls onto ungreased baking sheets. Bake at 350 degrees for 10 minutes; cool on wire rack. Makes 3 to 4 dozen.

It's in the mail! Drop cookies travel best...be sure to wrap the batch in aluminum foil and pack closely together to minimize shifting.

# Cookies

## Raisin Crunch Cookies in a Jar

*These hearty cookies are packed with plenty of good-for-you stuff!*

1-1/4 c. all-purpose flour
1 t. baking soda
1 t. baking powder
1/2 t. cinnamon
1/2 c. sugar
1/2 c. raisins

1-1/4 c. flaked coconut
1 c. corn flake cereal, crushed
3/4 c. brown sugar, packed
1/2 c. quick-cooking oats,
   uncooked

Sift together flour, baking soda, baking powder and cinnamon; set aside. In a one-quart, wide-mouth jar, layer sugar, raisins, coconut, corn flake cereal, brown sugar and oats, packing down after each addition. Top with flour mixture and secure lid. Tie on instructions.

## Instructions:

Empty cookie mix into a large mixing bowl; stir to combine. Add one cup softened butter, one slightly beaten egg and one teaspoon vanilla extract; mix until completely blended. Roll dough into walnut-size balls; place on a lightly greased baking sheet. Bake at 350 degrees for 10 to 12 minutes until edges are golden. Cool 5 minutes on baking sheet; remove to wire rack to cool completely. Makes 3 to 4 dozen.

Keep an eye out for
vintage jars at
flea markets,
garage sales and
antique shops.
Old-fashioned canning
jars make mixes
even more special!

# Peanut Butter Cookie Mix

*This classic is a welcome surprise for any season!*

1-1/2 c. all-purpose flour
1 t. baking powder
1/2 t. salt

1 c. brown sugar, packed
1-1/2 c. powdered sugar
3/4 c. baking cocoa

Sift together flour, baking powder and salt; set aside. Layer brown sugar, powdered sugar and cocoa in a one-quart, wide-mouth jar, wiping the inside of the jar with a paper towel after each addition to remove excess; firmly pack. Top with flour mixture and secure lid. Attach instructions to the jar.

## Instructions:

Empty cookie mix into a large mixing bowl, using your hands to thoroughly blend. Add 1/2 cup softened butter, 1/2 cup creamy peanut butter, one slightly beaten egg and one teaspoon vanilla extract; mix until completely blended. Shape dough into walnut-size balls; place on lightly greased baking sheets. Press balls down with a fork. Bake at 350 degrees for 9 to 11 minutes. Cool 5 minutes on baking sheet; transfer to a wire rack to cool completely. Makes 3 dozen.

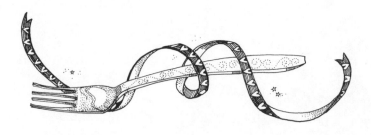

Tie on a dainty fork or cookie stamp to this mix.
Add a label with instructions to
"Make these cookies when pressed for time!"

# Cookies

## Slice & Bake Sugar Cookies

*Know a busy mom or two? This will make their day!*

| | |
|---|---|
| 2 c. margarine | 1 t. lemon extract |
| 2 c. sugar | 6 c. all-purpose flour |
| 3 eggs | 1 t. baking soda |
| 2 t. vanilla extract | 1/2 t. cinnamon |

In a large bowl, cream margarine and sugar together; beat in eggs, vanilla and lemon extract until light and fluffy. In a separate bowl, combine flour, baking soda and cinnamon. Gradually stir flour mixture into egg mixture until blended. Divide dough into 4 equal pieces; shape each piece into an 8 to 10-inch roll. Wrap each roll in wax paper or plastic wrap; freeze. Wrap each frozen dough roll in aluminum foil and again with printed fabric, if desired. Attach baking instructions. Makes 4 rolls.

## Instructions:

Store dough in refrigerator until ready to bake. Cut chilled dough into 1/4-inch slices; place on lightly greased baking sheets. Bake at 350 degrees for 8 to 10 minutes or until edges are golden. Makes 3 dozen.

Slice 'n Bake Sugar Cookie Dough

Give a roll of sugar cookies with the decorations included. Yummy chocolate-dipped raisins, bright sparkly sugars and sprinkles make cookie-baking fun!

# Cranberry-Orange Drops

*Tart and tangy with just enough sweetness!*

1/2 c. sugar
1/2 c. brown sugar, packed
1/4 c. butter, softened
1 egg
3 T. orange juice
1/2 t. orange extract

1 t. orange zest
1-1/2 c. all-purpose flour
1/2 t. baking powder
1/4 t. baking soda
1/2 t. salt
1 c. sweetened, dried cranberries

Cream together sugars and butter; stir in egg, orange juice, orange extract and orange zest. Sift together flour, baking powder, baking soda and salt; stir into orange mixture. Fold in cranberries. Drop dough by heaping teaspoonfuls on lightly greased baking sheets; bake at 375 degrees for 10 to 12 minutes. Remove from baking sheets to cool on wire racks. Makes 3 dozen.

Welcome a new family to the neighborhood! Fill a paper cone with cookies, treats and candy and hang it on the front door with ribbon.

# Cookies

## Ginger-Molasses Cookies

*Yummy gingerbread flavor without the work!*

2-1/2 c. all-purpose flour
2 t. ground ginger
1 t. cinnamon
2 t. baking soda
1/2 t. salt

3/4 c. butter, softened
1 c. brown sugar, packed
1 egg
1/3 c. molasses
1/2 c. sugar

Combine flour, ginger, cinnamon, baking soda and salt. In a separate bowl, beat together butter and brown sugar until light and fluffy; beat in egg and molasses. Gradually add flour mixture just until mixed. Chill dough until firm, about one hour. Shape chilled dough into one-inch balls, roll in sugar and place on ungreased baking sheets. Bake at 350 degrees for 15 minutes or until golden. Cool on baking sheets for 2 minutes, then move to wire racks to completely cool. Makes 6 dozen.

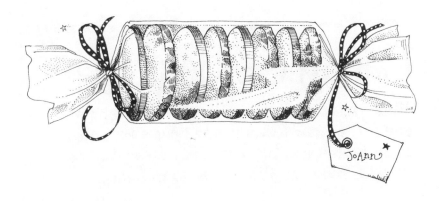

Hosting a dinner party? Stack a few cookies at each place setting and tie up with gingham ribbon...a sweet surprise for each guest.

# Candy Cookies in a Jar

*A great pick-me-up for a friend under the weather.*

2-1/2 c. all-purpose flour
1 t. salt
1 t. baking soda
1 t. vanilla powder

3/4 c. brown sugar, packed
3/4 c. sugar
1-1/2 c. candy-coated chocolates

Sift together flour, salt, baking soda and vanilla powder; set aside. In a one-quart, wide-mouth jar, layer flour mixture, brown sugar and sugar, packing down tightly after each addition. Fill remainder of jar with candy-coated chocolates and secure lid. Attach a gift tag with instructions.

## Instructions:

Pour jar contents into a large mixing bowl; blend in 2 eggs and one cup shortening. Drop tablespoonfuls onto ungreased baking sheets; bake at 350 degrees for 8 to 10 minutes. Makes 2 dozen.

## Candy Cookies in a Jar

Pour jar contents into a large bowl; blend in 2 eggs, 1 teaspoon vanilla and 1 cup shortening. Drop tablespoonfuls onto ungreased baking sheets. Bake at 350° for 8-10 minutes.

★ Makes 2 dozen. ★

Here's your instruction tag to copy & tie on.

# Cookies

## Sweet Cookie Bouquet

*Use sand to secure these pops in a whimsical pail.*

1 c. plus 2 T. cake flour
1/2 t. baking soda
1/2 c. sugar
1/2 c. brown sugar, packed
1/2 c. butter, softened
1/4 t. salt

1 egg, beaten
1 t. vanilla extract
1 c. semi-sweet chocolate chips
1/2 c. chopped pecans
1/4 c. flaked coconut
36 lollipop sticks

Combine flour and baking soda in a small bowl; set aside. In a separate bowl, cream sugars and butter until light and fluffy. Add salt, egg and vanilla, beating well. Gradually add flour mixture, stirring until combined. Fold in chocolate chips, pecans and coconut. Drop by heaping teaspoonfuls onto baking sheets lined with aluminum foil. Push a lollipop stick about two-thirds of the way into each cookie; gently press dough around stick to seal. Bake at 375 degrees for 8 to 10 minutes; cool on pan for 30 minutes before removing with a spatula. Wrap each cookie in plastic wrap and tie with a ribbon to secure. Makes 3 dozen.

National Boss' Day is October 16th...surprise the boss with a Sweet Cookie Bouquet!

# Master Cookie Mix

*Attach a gift card with recipes for Lemony Sugar Cookies, Coconut Bites and Best Chocolate Chip Cookies...this mix makes all three!*

5 c. all-purpose flour
3-3/4 c. sugar
2 T. baking powder

1-1/2 t. salt
1-1/2 c. plus 2 T. butter,
   softened

Combine flour, sugar, baking powder and salt in a large bowl. Cut in butter until mixture resembles coarse crumbs. Store in an airtight container in refrigerator. Makes 10 cups.

Pass it on! Pack a cookie jar with a plastic zipping bag full of this easy mix for new moms, college students and newlyweds...don't forget to include the recipes too.

# Cookies

### Lemony Sugar Cookies:

4 c. Master Cookie Mix
1 egg
1-1/2 T. lemon zest

2 T. lemon juice
Garnish: sugar

Combine cookie mix, egg, lemon zest and lemon juice in a large bowl; mix well. Divide dough in half and shape each into a roll; wrap and chill for one hour. Cut rolls into 1/8-inch slices; place on greased baking sheets. Bake at 350 degrees for 8 minutes; cool on wire rack. Makes 4 dozen.

### Coconut Bites:

3 c. Master Cookie Mix
2 eggs
1 T. lemon zest
1 c. flaked coconut

3/4 c. chopped pecans
1/2 c. red candied cherries,
   chopped
Garnish: sugar

Mix together cookie mix, eggs and lemon zest; stir in coconut, pecans and cherries. Spread mixture in a well-greased 13"x9" baking pan. Bake at 350 degrees for 20 to 25 minutes or until center springs back when lightly pressed. While warm, cut into squares and sprinkle with sugar. Makes 4 to 5 dozen.

### Best Chocolate Chip Cookies:

2 c. Master Cookie Mix
1/2 c. brown sugar, packed
1 egg

1 t. vanilla extract
1 c. semi-sweet chocolate chips
1/2 c. chopped walnuts

Combine cookie mix, brown sugar, egg and vanilla; stir in chocolate chips and nuts. Drop by rounded teaspoonfuls onto greased baking sheets. Bake at 375 degrees for 12 to 15 minutes or until golden; cool on wire rack. Makes 3 dozen.

# Irish Shortbread Mix

*Crunchy and rich, this mix is so easy!*

1-1/2 c. all-purpose flour        1/8 t. salt
3/4 c. powdered sugar

Combine all ingredients, blending well. Store in an airtight container. Attach a gift tag and instructions.

## Instructions:

Knead one cup softened butter into shortbread mix; firmly press mixture into an 8" pie plate. Bake at 300 degrees for one hour. Cut in wedges while warm. Makes one dozen.

Surprise a friend with a little luck o' the Irish...dress up a tin of shortbread mix with a bright green and white ribbon for St. Patrick's Day!

# Cookies

## Happy Birthday Cookies

*Spell out a friend's name for a birthday surprise!*

| | |
|---|---|
| 3/4 c. butter, softened | 1-1/2 t. almond extract |
| 1 c. powdered sugar | 2-1/2 c. all-purpose flour |
| 1 egg | 1/8 t. salt |

Cream butter and sugar in a large bowl until fluffy. Add egg and almond extract; beat until smooth. In a separate bowl, combine flour and salt; add to creamed mixture, stirring until a soft dough forms. Divide dough in half, wrap in plastic wrap and chill one hour. On a lightly floured surface, roll dough to 1/4-inch thickness. Use alphabet cookie cutters to cut out "Happy Birthday" cookies; place on greased baking sheets. Bake at 350 degrees for 8 to 10 minutes; place cookies on a wire rack, with wax paper underneath, to cool. Spoon icing over letters and allow to harden. Makes about 5 sets of cookies.

### Icing:

| | |
|---|---|
| 1/4 c. water | 1-1/4 t. almond extract |
| 2 T. corn syrup | 2 to 3 t. whipping cream |
| 4 c. powdered sugar | Optional: food coloring |

Combine water and corn syrup in a heavy saucepan. Add sugar, stirring until well blended; use a pastry brush to scrape down any sugar on sides of pan. Cook over medium to low heat until candy thermometer reaches 100 degrees; remove from heat. Stir in almond extract and 2 teaspoons cream; cool 5 minutes. Divide icing into small bowls and color, if desired. Add remaining cream for desired consistency.

# Orange Slice Cookies in a Jar

*Chewy orange candy in every bite!*

3/4 c. sugar
1/2 c. brown sugar, packed
1-3/4 c. all-purpose flour
1 t. baking powder

1/2 t. baking soda
1 t. orange zest
1/2 c. orange slice candies,
    quartered

In a one-quart, wide-mouth jar, layer the first 2 ingredients, packing down tightly. Combine flour, baking powder, baking soda and zest in a small bowl; add to jar. Wrap orange candies in plastic wrap; place on top of flour mix and secure lid. Tie on baking instructions.

## Instructions:

Remove candies from jar and set aside. Empty cookie mix in a large mixing bowl; stir to combine. Add 1/2 cup softened butter, one slightly beaten egg and one teaspoon vanilla extract; mix until blended. Stir in orange candies. Roll dough into walnut-size balls and place on a lightly greased baking sheet. Bake in a 375-degree oven for 12 to 14 minutes. Cool 5 minutes on baking sheet; transfer to wire rack to cool completely. Makes 2-1/2 dozen.

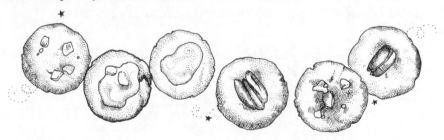

# Cookies

## Tropical Cookie Mix

*Just add sun for a get-away that can't be beat.*

| | |
|---|---|
| 1/3 c. sugar | 2 c. all-purpose flour |
| 1/2 c. brown sugar, packed | 1 t. baking soda |
| 1/3 c. flaked coconut | 1 t. baking powder |
| 2/3 c. chopped macadamia nuts | 1/8 t. salt |
| 2/3 c. chopped dates | |

Layer first 5 ingredients in a one-quart, wide-mouth jar in the order listed. Pack tightly between each layer. Combine flour, baking soda, baking powder and salt in a small bowl; add to jar. Secure lid and attach baking instructions.

## Instructions:

Empty cookie mix in a large bowl; stir to combine. Add 1/2 cup softened butter, one slightly beaten egg and one teaspoon vanilla extract; mix until completely blended. Roll dough into walnut-size balls; place on greased baking sheets. Press each cookie down slightly with the heel of your hand. Bake at 350 degrees for 11 to 13 minutes; cool 5 minutes on baking sheet. Move to wire rack to cool completely. Makes 2-1/2 dozen.

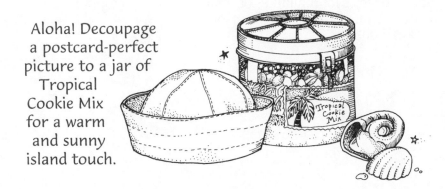

Aloha! Decoupage a postcard-perfect picture to a jar of Tropical Cookie Mix for a warm and sunny island touch.

# Spumoni Cookie Squares

*Just as yummy as the ice cream!*

1 c. butter
1-1/2 c. powdered sugar
1 egg
2 t. vanilla extract
2-1/2 c. all-purpose flour
1/2 c. mini semi-sweet chocolate
    chips, divided

2 drops green food coloring
1/2 c. pistachios, chopped
1 drop red food coloring
1/4 c. candied cherries, finely
    chopped

Cream together butter and sugar; beat in egg and vanilla. Gradually beat in flour until just blended. Shape dough into a brick and cut into three equal parts. Melt 2-1/2 tablespoons mini chocolate chips; cool. Flatten one portion dough, smooth melted chocolate over top and carefully knead until blended. Knead in remaining chips; roll dough into a 24-inch rope and flatten to 1/2-inch thickness. Flatten second portion dough; add green food color and knead to blend. Knead in chopped pistachios. Roll dough into a 24-inch rope, flatten and place on chocolate layer. Repeat with third dough portion, kneading in red food color, then cherries. Roll dough into a 24-inch rope, flatten and place on pistachio layer. Cut into two, 12-inch blocks, squaring off sides as much as possible. Wrap and chill until firm. Cut dough crosswise in 1/4-inch thick slices. Place on ungreased baking sheets. Bake at 375 degrees for 8 minutes or until puffed. Remove to wire rack to cool. Makes 5 dozen.

Pack Spumoni Cookie Squares
in pint-size canning jars
or stack them up in old-fashioned
sundae glasses.

# Cookies

## Chocolate-Cherry Cookies

*Bite-size cheer, these mini-fruitcake cookies are great for mailing.*

3/4 c. butter, softened
3/4 c. sugar
2 eggs
1 t. vanilla extract
2  1-oz. sqs. semi-sweet baking
   chocolate, melted
2-1/4 c. all-purpose flour
1 t. baking powder

1 c. candied red and green
   cherries, chopped
1/2 c. chopped pecans, toasted
1/2 c. chopped walnuts, toasted
1/2 c. semi-sweet chocolate
   chips
1 t. shortening

Cream butter and sugar in a large bowl until fluffy; add eggs and vanilla, beating until smooth. Stir in melted chocolate. In a separate bowl, combine flour and baking powder; add to creamed mixture to form a soft dough. Fold in cherries, pecans and walnuts. Drop by tablespoonfuls on lightly greased baking sheets; bake at 375 degrees for 6 to 8 minutes. Move to a wire rack to cool. Melt chocolate chips and shortening together in a double boiler, stirring continuously. Drizzle glaze over cooled cookies. Makes 4 to 5 dozen.

A tin filled with favorite Christmas cookies is extra special when the recipes are included!

# Crunch & Munch Cookies

*Try different candy bar pieces for a personalized cookie.*

1-1/2 c. all-purpose flour
1/2 t. baking soda
1/4 t. salt
1/2 c. margarine
3/4 c. brown sugar, packed

1 egg
1 t. vanilla extract
5  1.4-oz. chocolate-covered
    toffee candy bars, crushed
1/3 c. chopped pecans

Combine flour, baking soda and salt; set aside. In a separate bowl, cream margarine, sugar, egg and vanilla; gradually stir in flour mixture. Blend in toffee bars and nuts. Drop by tablespoonfuls on greased baking sheets; bake at 350 degrees for 12 to 15 minutes. Makes 2 dozen.

A clever party favor! Pack chunky, chewy cookies in clear cellophane bags...fold top over, punch 2 holes with a hole-punch and weave in ribbon.

# Cookies

## Oatmeal-Raisin Cookie Mix

*Everyone loves these chewy classics!*

3/4 c. brown sugar, packed
1/2 c. sugar
3/4 c. raisins
2 c. quick-cooking oats,
   uncooked

1 c. all-purpose flour
1-1/4 t. cinnamon
1/2 t. nutmeg
1 t. baking soda
1/4 t. salt

Place brown sugar in a one-quart, wide-mouth jar. Layer sugar, raisins and oats on top, packing after each addition. Combine remaining ingredients in a small bowl and pour into jar. Secure lid and attach baking instructions.

## Instructions:

Empty cookie mix into a large bowl; stir to combine. Add 3/4 cup softened butter, one slightly beaten egg and one teaspoon vanilla extract; blend well. Shape into walnut-size balls and place on lightly greased baking sheets. Bake at 350 degrees for 11 to 13 minutes or until edges are golden; move to wire racks to cool. Makes 3 dozen.

Make a personalized gift for a friend or neighbor! Place a jar of Oatmeal-Raisin Cookie Mix in a muslin bag...stencil the outside with their initial. So thoughtful!

# Chocolate-Covered Raisin Cookie Mix

*Just like the candy at the movie theater...yum!*

| | |
|---|---|
| 1-3/4 c. all-purpose flour | 3/4 c. sugar |
| 1 t. baking powder | 1/2 c. brown sugar, packed |
| 1/2 t. baking soda | 1 c. chocolate-covered raisins |
| 1/8 t. salt | 1/2 c. milk chocolate chips |

Combine flour, baking powder, baking soda and salt in a mixing bowl; set aside. Layer remaining ingredients in a one-quart, wide-mouth jar. Top with flour mixture and secure lid. Attach a tag with instructions.

## Instructions:

Empty cookie mix into a large mixing bowl; stir to combine. Add 1/2 cup softened butter, one slightly beaten egg and one teaspoon vanilla extract; mix until blended. Shape dough into walnut-size balls; place on parchment-lined baking sheets. Bake at 375 degrees for 13 to 15 minutes; cool 5 minutes on baking sheet then move to wire rack. Makes 2-1/2 dozen.

Cookie baking with all the fun and no fuss! Place a jar of Chocolate-Covered Raisin Cookie Mix on a baking sheet. Add a bag of chocolate chips and a bag of chocolate-covered raisins...tie it all up with a tea towel and wide ribbon and surprise a busy mom.

# Cookies

## Peanut Butter Cup Cookie Mix

*Peanut butter lovers won't be able to resist.*

3/4 c. sugar
1/2 c. brown sugar, packed
1-3/4 c. all-purpose flour
1 t. baking powder

1/2 t. baking soda
20 mini peanut butter cups,
   chopped

Layer sugar and brown sugar in a one-quart, wide-mouth jar. Combine flour, baking powder and baking soda in a small mixing bowl; pour into jar, packing down tightly. Add peanut butter cups. Secure lid and attach instructions.

### Instructions:

Remove peanut butter cups from jar and set aside. Empty remaining contents into a large mixing bowl; blend. Add 1/2 cup softened butter, one slightly beaten egg and one teaspoon vanilla; mix until completely blended. Stir in peanut butter cups. Shape dough into walnut-size balls and place on greased baking sheets. Bake at 375 degrees for 12 to 14 minutes; cool 5 minutes on sheet before removing to wire rack to cool completely. Makes 2-1/2 dozen.

Celebrate Best Friends' Day on June 8th with a jar of Peanut Butter Cup Cookie Mix with a half gallon of vanilla ice cream. Dig in and chat the afternoon away!

# Key Lime Bites

*The taste of that oh-so-refreshing pie in a cookie!*

3/4 c. butter, softened
1 c. powdered sugar, divided
2 T. lime juice
zest of 2 limes
1 T. vanilla extract

1-3/4 c. plus 2 T. all-purpose
    flour
2 T. cornstarch
1/2 t. salt

Cream butter and 1/3 cup powdered sugar until fluffy. Blend in lime juice, zest and vanilla; set aside. In a separate bowl, whisk together flour, cornstarch and salt; add to butter mixture, stirring until combined. Roll dough into a log shape and chill for one hour. Slice log into 1/8-inch thick rounds; place on parchment-lined baking sheets. Bake at 350 degrees for 11 to 14 minutes or until slightly golden. Place remaining powdered sugar in a large plastic bag. Remove cookies from oven and allow to cool for several minutes. While still warm, place cookies in bag with powdered sugar; toss gently to coat. Makes 2 dozen.

Wrap rolls of cookie dough in foil and cover with an extra layer of fun fabric...tie it all up with fancy ribbon or retro rick-rack. Attach the baking instructions and give to a friend with a sweet tooth just because!

# Cookies

## Creamy Orange Cookie Mix

*Just like a Creamsicle!*

| | |
|---|---|
| 1/2 c. orange drink mix | 1-3/4 c. all-purpose flour |
| 3/4 c. sugar | 1/2 t. baking soda |
| 1-1/2 c. vanilla chips | 1/2 t. baking powder |
| 1 t. orange zest | |

Layer first 4 ingredients in a one-quart, wide-mouth jar; pack tightly after each addition. Combine flour, baking soda and baking powder in a small bowl; place in jar on top. Secure lid and attach instructions.

## Instructions:

Pour cookie mix in a large bowl; stir to combine. Add 1/2 cup softened butter, one slightly beaten egg and one teaspoon vanilla extract; blend well. Roll dough into one-inch balls; place on lightly greased baking sheets. Bake at 375 degrees for 12 to 14 minutes or until tops are lightly golden. Cool 5 minutes on baking sheet, then move to wire rack to cool completely. Makes 2 to 3 dozen.

Create a custom mix by painting on initials with etching cream to a clear glass jar. Try adding a rubber-stamped etching too!

# Jumbo Fortune Cookies

*Good fortune is sure to smile on you when you give these cookies!*

4 egg whites
1 c. super fine sugar
1 c. all-purpose flour, sifted
1/8 t. salt

1/4 c. plus 1 T. butter, melted
3 T. whipping cream
1 t. almond extract

Write fortunes on strips of paper about 4" long and 1/2" wide. Beat together egg whites and sugar; add flour and salt, mixing well. Blend in remaining ingredients. Pour one tablespoon batter onto half of a baking sheet coated with non-stick vegetable spray; spread with a spoon into a 5-inch circle. Repeat on other half. Bake at 400 degrees for 8 minutes or until edges turn golden. Working quickly, slide a spatula under cookies; lift and place on a dish towel. Place a fortune on each cookie, close to the middle. Fold cookies in half, pinching at top to form a loose semicircle. Place the folded edge across the rim of a measuring cup and pull the pointed edges down, one on the inside of the cup and one on the outside; allow to harden. Repeat with remaining batter. Makes 15.

Instead of fortune-filled cookies, place different clues
inside each one letting friends know where
a grand gift may be hidden!

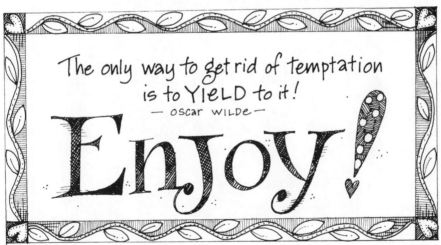

The only way to get rid of temptation is to YIELD to it!
— OSCAR WILDE —

Enjoy!

1. Copy   2. Color   3. Cut Out!

My Favorite Cookie MIX
in the whole, wide WONDERFUL world!

Homemade Cookies!
from:

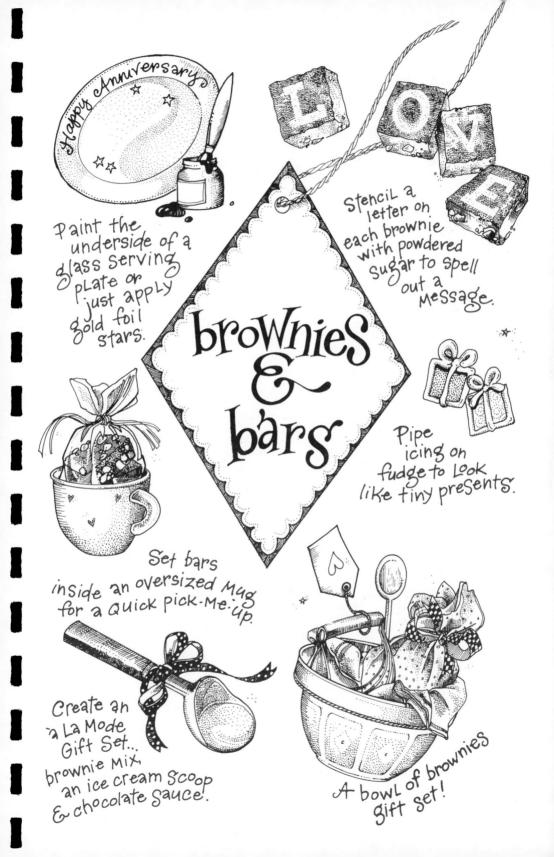

Paint the underside of a glass serving plate or just apply gold foil stars.

Stencil a letter on each brownie with powdered sugar to spell out a message.

# brownies & bars

Pipe icing on fudge to look like tiny presents.

Set bars inside an oversized mug for a quick pick-me-up.

Create an à La Mode Gift Set... brownie mix, an ice cream scoop & chocolate sauce.

A bowl of brownies gift set!

enjoy!

# Chocolatey Peppermint Brownies

*Squares of wax paper are perfect for individually wrapping these minty brownies.*

2 1-oz. sqs. unsweetened
   baking chocolate
1/3 c. butter
1 c. sugar
2 eggs
1 t. vanilla extract
3/4 c. all-purpose flour

1/2 t. baking powder
1/4 t. salt
1/3 c. chopped walnuts
2 1-oz. sqs. white baking
   chocolate
2 T. peppermint candies, crushed

Place chocolate and butter in a microwave-safe bowl; microwave on high for 2 minutes, stirring every 30 seconds until chocolate is melted. Beat in sugar, eggs and vanilla. Add flour, baking powder and salt; stir until smooth. Fold in nuts; pour batter into an 8"x8" glass dish coated with non-stick vegetable spray. Rotating dish twice during baking, microwave on medium-high for 7 to 9 minutes or until inserted toothpick comes out clean. Let cool completely. Place white baking chocolate in a microwave-safe bowl; microwave on high for 1-1/2 minutes, stirring every 30 seconds. Drizzle white chocolate over cooled brownies; sprinkle with peppermint candies. Serves 10 to 12.

Decorate a paper sack with stencils or rubber stamps and fill with brownies. Fold the top over, punch 2 holes and slide a peppermint stick through for a sweet gift bag.

# Brownies & Bars

## Cool & Creamy Fudge Bars

*Cut with seasonal cookie cutters for a festive treat!*

4  1-oz. sqs. unsweetened
   baking chocolate
1/2 c. plus 2 T. butter, divided
2 c. sugar
4 eggs, divided
2 t. vanilla extract
1 c. all-purpose flour

8-oz. pkg. cream cheese,
   softened
1 T. cornstarch
14-oz. can sweetened condensed
   milk
1 t. peppermint extract

Melt chocolate with 1/2 cup butter in a double boiler. Combine chocolate mixture, sugar, 3 eggs, vanilla and flour in a large mixing bowl; spread in a greased 13"x9" baking pan. Bake at 350 degrees for 12 minutes. While brownie layer is in oven, blend cream cheese, remaining butter and cornstarch until fluffy. Gradually beat in milk, peppermint extract and remaining egg; pour over brownie layer. Bake at 350 degrees for 30 minutes or until set. Top with glaze. Cool completely, chill and cut into bars. Makes 15 to 18 servings.

## Glaze:

1 c. semi-sweet chocolate chips    1/2 c. whipping cream

Combine ingredients in a small saucepan; melt over low heat, stirring until thickened.

For a St. Patty's Day treasure, add green food coloring to the cream cheese layer...wrap up in green cellophane and toss in a handful of gold-wrapped chocolate coins.

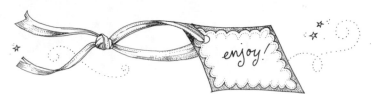

# Butterscotch Brownie Mix

*These rich brownies are the perfect gift for any occasion.*

2 c. all-purpose flour
1-1/2 T. baking powder
1/8 t. salt

1/2 c. butterscotch chips
3/4 c. chopped pecans
2 c. brown sugar, packed

Combine flour, baking powder and salt. In a one-quart, wide-mouth jar, layer coconut, pecans and brown sugar, packing down as tightly as possible. Add flour mixture, pressing down to pack. Seal with jar lid and attach instructions.

## Instructions:

Empty jar of mix into a large mixing bowl, stirring to blend. Add 3/4 cup butter, 2 slightly beaten eggs and 2 teaspoons vanilla extract; mix until completely blended. Spread batter into a greased 13"x9" baking pan. Bake at 375 degrees for 25 minutes. Cool in pan for 15 minutes before cutting into bars. Makes 2 dozen.

Tie on butterscotch candies to this brownie mix...just punch holes in the wrapper, thread on raffia and tie around the neck of the jar. Friends can enjoy these while brownies bake or crush them up and add to the mix!

# Brownies & Bars

## Creamiest Peanut Butter Fudge

*For extra-nutty flavor, try sprinkling chopped peanuts on top of the fudge immediately after pouring into the pan.*

4 c. sugar
1 c. brown sugar, packed
1/2 c. butter
12-oz. can evaporated milk

7-oz. jar marshmallow creme
16-oz. jar creamy peanut butter
1-1/2 t. vanilla extract

Combine sugars, butter and milk in a saucepan over medium heat. Bring to a boil, stirring constantly for 7 minutes; remove from heat. Stir in marshmallow creme until melted. Stir in peanut butter and vanilla until smooth. Pour mixture in a greased 13"x9" pan; cool and cut into squares. Makes 24 servings.

Start the day off right...brighten up everyone's Monday morning with a basket full of fudge. Co-workers will love nibbling all day long!

# Confetti Granola Bars

*So easy to make…a great gift for snack-lovers!*

4-1/2 c. quick-cooking oats,
  uncooked
1 c. all-purpose flour
1 t. baking soda
1 t. vanilla extract

2/3 c. butter, softened
1/2 c. honey
1/3 c. brown sugar, packed
2 c. candy-coated chocolates

In a large mixing bowl, combine all ingredients except candy-coated chocolates; mix well. Gently stir in candy-coated chocolates. Lightly press mixture into a greased 13"x9" pan. Bake at 325 degrees for 18 to 22 minutes or until golden. Let cool for 10 minutes; cut into bars. Let bars cool completely in pan before removing. Makes 10 to 12 servings.

A college student's dream! Fill airtight containers (look for containers in school colors) with cookies, brownies and bars. Send during exam week for a tasty study break.

## Chewy Peanut Bars

*The bars are so irresistible, you'll need to make two batches....one to give and one to keep!*

1-1/4 c. all-purpose flour
2/3 c. sugar
1/3 c. baking cocoa
1/4 c. brown sugar, packed
1 t. baking powder
1/8 t. salt

1/2 c. chilled butter
2 eggs, beaten
10-oz. pkg. peanut butter chips
14-oz. can sweetened condensed
   milk
1 c. flaked coconut

Combine first 6 ingredients in a large mixing bowl; cut in butter to resemble coarse crumbs. Add eggs, mixing well. Spread batter into a greased 13"x9" baking pan; bake at 350 degrees for 8 minutes. Remove from oven; top evenly with peanut butter chips, milk and coconut. Return to oven for 20 minutes or until golden; cool. Makes 2 to 3 dozen bars.

For a simple (and tasty!) garnish for cookie bars, melt 1/2 cup semi-sweet chocolate chips with 1-1/2 teaspoons shortening. Drizzle over bars before cutting and watch the treats disappear. Try mint, raspberry and white chocolate chips too...yum!

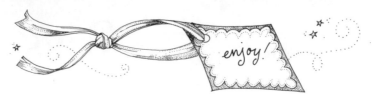

# Pineapple-Cherry Fudge

*An oh-so-refreshing twist on traditional fudge.*

1 c. evaporated milk
3 c. sugar
2 T. butter

1 c. crushed pineapple, drained
2 t. lemon juice
Garnish: maraschino cherries

Combine milk, sugar and butter in a saucepan; bring to a boil. Stirring constantly, add pineapple and cook over medium heat to soft-ball stage, or 234 to 243 degrees on a candy thermometer, about 25 minutes. Remove from heat and cool. Stir in lemon juice; beat until mixture is smooth and no longer shiny. Turn into a buttered 9"x9" pan; lightly press cherries about one to 1-1/2 inches apart into fudge. Let cool and cut into squares centering a cherry in each square. Makes about 2 dozen squares.

A tropical twist...place Pineapple-Cherry Fudge in a colorful bowl, wrap with cellophane and tie with a lei.

# Brownies & Bars

## Seaside Brownie Mix

*Postcards from favorite vacation spots make great gift tags!*

1/3 c. chopped walnuts
1/2 c. semi-sweet chocolate
   chips
1/3 c. flaked coconut

2/3 c. brown sugar, packed
3/4 c. sugar
1/3 c. baking cocoa
1-1/2 c. all-purpose flour

In a one-quart, wide-mouth jar, layer first 5 ingredients in the order listed, packing tightly after each addition. Add cocoa, pack down, then wipe the inside of the jar with a paper towel to remove any excess; add flour, packing tightly. Secure lid; tie on instructions.

## Instructions:

In a medium bowl, combine 2 eggs, 2/3 cup oil and 2 teaspoons vanilla extract; mix well. Gradually stir in jar contents and blend well. Spread into a greased 8"x8" baking pan. Bake at 350 degrees for 30 minutes or until an inserted toothpick comes out clean. Makes 10 to 12 servings.

A summertime treat! Give a sand bucket filled with Seaside Brownie Mix, a beach towel and sun block lotion.

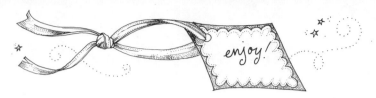

*enjoy!*

# Chocolatey Butterscotch Squares

*Just as tasty with milk chocolate chips too!*

1-1/2 c. graham cracker crumbs
14-oz. can sweetened condensed
   milk
1-1/2 c. semi-sweet chocolate
   chips

1 c. butterscotch chips
1 c. chopped walnuts

Mix together all ingredients in a medium mixing bowl. Line a
9"x9" baking pan with aluminum foil and grease foil; press mixture in
pan. Bake at 350 degrees for 30 to 35 minutes. Cool for 45 minutes,
remove from pan and peel off foil. Cut into squares. Makes
2 dozen squares.

Sweets for a sweetheart! Cut out bars with cookie cutters and
pipe chocolatey x's and o's on top.

# Brownies & Bars

## Sunny Day Brownies

*A welcome treat for any chocolate-lover.*

2 c. all-purpose flour
1/4 t. baking soda
1 t. baking powder
3/4 t. salt
2/3 c. butter, melted

2 c. brown sugar, packed
2 eggs
2 t. vanilla extract
1 c. mini milk chocolate chips
3/4 c. chopped walnuts

Combine flour, baking soda, baking powder and salt in a large mixing bowl; set aside. In a separate bowl, blend butter and brown sugar together; mix in eggs and vanilla. Add flour mixture, stirring to blend. Spread batter into a lightly greased 13"x9" baking pan. Sprinkle with chocolate chips and nuts. Bake at 350 degrees for 30 minutes; cool in pan and cut into bars. Makes 12 to 15 bars.

Friends visiting this summer? Welcome them early with a batch of Sunny Day Brownies...attach a pair of jaunty plastic sunglasses to them when mailing. Use acrylic paint to write a message on the lenses!

## Nutty Apricot Bars

*These bars make a delightful hostess gift.*

1-1/2 c. all-purpose flour,
    divided
1/4 c. sugar
1/2 c. butter
2/3 c. dried apricots, minced
2 eggs, beaten

1 c. brown sugar, packed
1 t. vanilla extract
1/4 t. salt
1/2 t. baking powder
1/2 c. chopped pecans
Garnish: powdered sugar

Combine one cup flour, sugar and butter. Pat into a lightly greased 11"x7" pan; bake at 350 degrees for 12 minutes. Cover apricots with hot water and simmer until water is gone; set aside to cool. In a medium bowl, combine eggs, brown sugar, vanilla, salt, baking powder and remaining flour, mixing well; add apricots and chopped nuts. Spread mixture on baked crust. Bake at 350 degrees for 30 minutes. Sprinkle with powdered sugar and cut into bars. Makes one dozen.

Celebrate Sisters' Day on August 5th! Fill a basket with yummy treats in her favorite flavors...top with ribbon curled into a pretty bow for a quick & easy surprise!

# Brownies & Bars

## Homemade Apple Butter Bars

*No one can resist the rich taste of apple butter blended with brown sugar.*

1 c. brown sugar, packed
1-1/2 c. all-purpose flour
3/4 c. butter
1-1/2 c. quick-cooking oats, uncooked

1/2 t. baking soda
1 t. almond extract
1/2 t. salt
1-1/2 c. apple butter

Mix all ingredients, except apple butter, until crumbly. Spread half the mixture in a lightly greased 13"x9" pan. Spread apple butter on top; cover with remaining crumb mixture. Bake at 350 degrees for 20 to 25 minutes; cool and cut into squares. Makes 12 to 15 servings.

A sweet surprise to welcome harvest! Arrange Homemade Apple Butter Bars on a brand new cutting board...cover it all with festive cellophane and tie with raffia.

# Lemon Delights

*A burst of sunshine in every bite!*

1 c. all-purpose flour
1/2 c. margarine, softened
1/2 c. chopped pecans
2 T. sugar
2  3.4 oz. pkgs. instant lemon
    pudding mix

3 c. cold milk
2-1/2 c. frozen whipped topping,
    thawed
8-oz. pkg. cream cheese
1-1/4 c. powdered sugar
Optional: 1/2 c. pecan halves

Combine first 4 ingredients to make a dough; press into a lightly greased 13"x9" baking pan. Bake at 350 degrees for 15 minutes; cool completely. Mix together pudding mix and milk until thickened; spread over cooled crust. Combine remaining ingredients until smooth; spread over pudding layer. Sprinkle top with pecan halves, if desired. Chill at least 4 hours before serving. Makes one dozen.

A real pick-me-up when life gives you lemons! Deliver Lemon Delights along with a cheerful new pitcher already filled with lemons and plenty of sugar.

# Brownies & Bars

## Orange-Macadamia Fudge

*A delicious way to let someone know you're thinking of them.*

1/2 c. butter, melted
1-1/2 c. sugar
5-oz. can evaporated milk
2 c. mini marshmallows

1 c. semi-sweet chocolate chips
3/4 c. chopped macadamia nuts
1 T. orange extract

Combine butter, sugar and milk in a microwave-safe bowl; cook on high for 8 minutes, stirring every 3 minutes. Immediately add marshmallows and chocolate chips, stirring until melted and smooth. Stir in nuts and orange extract. Pour into an 8"x8" pan lined with aluminum foil; chill until firm. Remove fudge from pan, peel away foil and cut into squares. Makes 2 pounds.

Dress up a box of fudge and hand-deliver to make someone feel extra special. Decoupage photos, glue on paper doilies and sprinkle with glitter...don't forget to include the recipe!

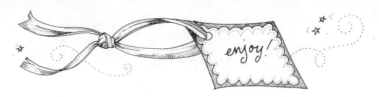

# Crispy Chocolate Chippers

*A favorite of kids and grown-ups alike!*

1 c. corn syrup
1 c. sugar
1-1/2 c. creamy peanut butter

8 c. crispy rice cereal
1 c. semi-sweet chocolate chips
1/2 c. peanuts, crushed

Combine corn syrup, sugar and peanut butter in a large microwave-safe bowl; microwave on high 2 to 3 minutes until boiling. Remove from microwave and stir in cereal, chocolate chips and peanuts. Pour mixture into a buttered 13"x9" pan. With damp hands, press down the treats until smoothed. Let cool and cut into squares. Makes 2 dozen.

Homemade coupons make great gifts for the whole family. How about a coupon volunteering to be a young teen's personal taxi service on a Friday night?

# Brownies & Bars

## Friendship Fudge

*Cut into stars with a mini cookie cutter for the 4th of July!*

1/2 c. powdered sugar
3-oz. pkg. cream cheese
16-oz. can vanilla frosting
2 c. white chocolate chips,
  melted
3/4 c. chopped walnuts

2/3 c. sweetened, dried
  cranberries
1 t. orange zest
Optional: 1/3 cup flaked
  coconut, toasted

Combine sugar, cream cheese and frosting in a medium mixing bowl, blending well; stir in remaining ingredients. Line a 9"x9" baking pan with aluminum foil and coat with non-stick vegetable spray; pour mixture into pan. Sprinkle coconut over the top, if desired. Chill for one hour or until firm; cut into squares. Makes 15 squares.

Spoon a little melted chocolate into the bottoms of candy cups, swirl, refrigerate and then carefully peel paper away for pretty (and yummy!) chocolate cups.

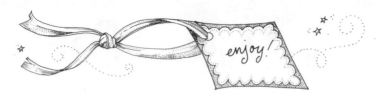

# Super Fudge Brownies in a Jar

*This gift is sure to bring lots of smiles!*

2 c. sugar
1 c. baking cocoa
1 c. all-purpose flour

1 c. chopped pecans
6-oz. pkg. semi-sweet chocolate chips

In a one-quart, wide-mouth jar, layer sugar and cocoa and pack down; wipe the inside of the jar with a paper towel to remove any excess from the sides. Layer flour, pecans and chocolate chips, packing down tightly after each addition. Secure lid and attach a gift tag with instructions.

## Instructions:

In a large bowl, cream one cup softened butter. Add 4 eggs, one at a time, beating well after each addition. Add brownie mix and beat until smooth. Spread into a greased 13"x9" baking pan; bake 40 to 50 minutes until an inserted toothpick comes out clean. Makes 18 servings.

How fun! Attach a small cape made of red felt to a jar of Super Fudge Brownies. Attach a tag reading "Chocolate emergency? Super Fudge Brownies to the rescue!"

# Brownies & Bars

## Chocolate-Covered Raisin Fudge

*Cut fudge into both small and large pieces to
please appetites of all sizes.*

1-1/2 c. sugar
2/3 c. evaporated milk
2 T. butter
1/4 t. salt
2 c. mini marshmallows
1-1/2 c. semi-sweet
   chocolate chips

2 c. chocolate-covered
   raisins, divided
1 t. vanilla extract
1/2 c. chopped nuts

Combine sugar, milk, butter and salt in a heavy saucepan; bring to a
rolling boil over medium heat, stirring constantly. Boil for 4 to
5 minutes and remove from heat. Stir in marshmallows, chocolate
chips, one cup raisins, vanilla and nuts. Stir continuously for one
minute until marshmallows are melted. Pour into an 8"x8" baking pan
lined with foil; cool for one minute. Sprinkle remaining raisins on top,
pressing in slightly. Chill for 2 hours until firm. Lift from pan and
remove foil. Cut into squares. Makes 1-1/2 dozen squares.

A stack of sweets!
Slice fudge into
various size
squares. Place a
small square on
top of a large and
wrap with
a licorice bow.

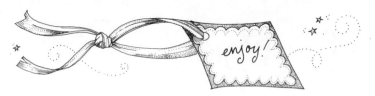

## Ooey-Gooey Fudge

*Better than any fudge you can buy!*

1/2 c. butter
1/3 c. baking cocoa
1/4 c. brown sugar, packed
1/4 c. milk
3-1/2 c. powdered sugar
1-1/2 t. vanilla extract

30 caramels, unwrapped
1 T. water
2 c. salted peanuts
1/2 c. semi-sweet chocolate
  chips
1/2 c. milk chocolate chips

In a microwave-safe bowl, combine butter, cocoa, brown sugar and milk; microwave on high for 3 minutes or until mixture begins to boil. Stir in powdered sugar and vanilla; pour into a greased 8"x8" pan. In a separate microwave-safe bowl, heat caramels and water on high for 2 minutes or until caramels melt; stir in peanuts. Spread mixture over chocolate layer. In a separate microwave-safe bowl, combine chocolate chips; microwave on high for one minute or until melted. Spread over caramel layer. Chill for 2 hours and cut into squares. Makes 32 squares.

Celebrate National Kids' Day on October 8th with this Ooey-Gooey Fudge. Share a tin with kids in the neighborhood or at church...be sure to include a big stack of napkins and lots of milk!

## Peanut Butter-Marbled Brownies

*Fresh-from-the-oven brownies are a treat everyone will love...be sure to keep lots of cold milk handy!*

2  3-oz. pkgs. cream cheese
1/2 c. creamy peanut butter
2-1/4 c. sugar, divided
4 eggs, divided
2 T. milk
1 c. butter, melted
2 t. vanilla extract

3/4 c. baking cocoa
1-1/4 c. all-purpose flour
1/2 t. baking powder
1/4 t. salt
6-oz. pkg. semi-sweet chocolate
   chips

In a medium bowl, beat cream cheese, peanut butter, 1/4 cup sugar, one egg and milk until smooth; set aside. In a separate bowl, mix together butter, remaining sugar and vanilla. Add in remaining eggs, one at a time, beating well after each addition. In a separate bowl, combine cocoa, flour, baking powder and salt; mix into batter. Fold in chocolate chips. Remove one cup of the chocolate batter. Spread the remaining batter into a greased 13"x9" baking pan; spread peanut butter filling on top. Drop the reserved chocolate batter by teaspoonfuls over the filling. Using a knife, gently swirl through the top layers for a marbled effect. Bake at 350 degrees for 35 to 40 minutes or until an inserted toothpick comes out almost clean. Cool and cut into squares. Makes 36.

Wrap brownies individually
in wax paper or
colored cellophane...handy
treats to give as
party favors or to co-workers.

# Rocky Road Fudge Bars

*Pile these ultra-fudgy bars into the back of a toy dump truck for a charming gift.*

3/4 c. butter, divided
1-oz. sq. unsweetened baking chocolate
1-1/2 c. sugar, divided
1 c. plus 2 T. all-purpose flour, divided
3/4 c. chopped walnuts, divided
1 t. baking powder
1-1/2 t. vanilla extract, divided
3 eggs, divided
6 oz. cream cheese

1 c. semi-sweet chocolate chips
2 c. mini marshmallows

## Topping:
1/4 c. butter
1-oz. sq. unsweetened baking chocolate
2 oz. cream cheese
1/4 c. milk
3 c. powdered sugar
1 t. vanilla extract

Melt 1/2 cup butter and chocolate over low heat. Add one cup sugar, one cup flour, 1/2 cup nuts, baking powder, one teaspoon vanilla extract and 2 eggs; mix well. Spread mixture in a greased and floured 13"x9" baking pan. Combine cream cheese, remaining butter, sugar, flour, vanilla and egg; beat until smooth and fluffy. Stir in remaining nuts; spread over chocolate mixture and sprinkle with chocolate chips. Bake at 350 degrees for 25 to 35 minutes until inserted toothpick comes out clean. Remove from oven, sprinkle with mini marshmallows and return to oven for 2 minutes. Melt topping ingredients together, stirring until smooth. Pour over bars; use a spoon to create a swirl pattern. Cool and cut into bars. Makes 36 bars.

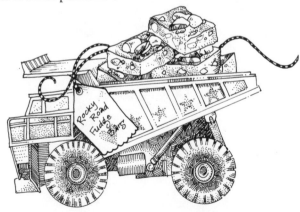

# Brownies & Bars

## Chewy Chocolate Chip Bars

*Great for packing in school lunches!*

2 c. semi-sweet chocolate
  chips, divided
1/2 c. butter
3 eggs

1-1/4 c. all-purpose flour
1 c. sugar
1 t. vanilla extract
1/4 t. baking soda

Melt one cup chips and butter in a large saucepan over low heat, stirring until smooth; remove from heat. Stir in eggs; add flour, sugar, vanilla and baking soda. Stir in remaining chocolate chips. Spread into a greased 13"x9" baking pan; bake at 350 degrees for 18 to 22 minutes or until inserted toothpick comes out slightly sticky. Cool completely in pan on wire rack. Makes 2 dozen.

An old-fashioned lunch box is a perfect container to fill with cookie bars and brownies...a great teacher gift too!

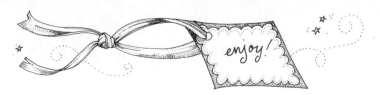

# 4-Layer Candy

*A perfect treat for Valentine's Day, Sweetest Day or any day!*

1 c. milk chocolate chips
1/4 c. butterscotch chips
1/2 c. creamy peanut butter,
    divided
1/4 c. butter, melted
1 c. sugar
1/4 c. evaporated milk

1-1/2 c. marshmallow creme
2 t. vanilla extract
1-1/2 c. salted, chopped peanuts
14-oz. pkg. caramels,
    unwrapped
1/4 c. whipping cream

In a small saucepan, combine chocolate chips, butterscotch chips and 1/4 cup peanut butter. Cook over low heat, stirring constantly, until melted and smooth. Pour into a lightly greased 13"x9" pan; refrigerate until set. In a heavy saucepan, combine melted butter, sugar and evaporated milk; bring to a boil and stir for 5 minutes. Remove pan from heat; stir in marshmallow creme, remaining peanut butter and vanilla. Fold in peanuts and spread over set chocolate layer; refrigerate until set. Combine caramels and whipping cream in a saucepan; stir over low heat until melted and smooth. Spread on top of set peanut layer; refrigerate until smooth. Pour frosting over caramel layer; refrigerate for one hour. Cut into one-inch squares. Makes 8 dozen.

## Frosting:

1 c. milk chocolate chips
1/4 c. butterscotch chips

1/4 c. creamy peanut butter

Combine all ingredients in a saucepan; stir over low heat until smooth.

# Brownies & Bars

## Double-the-Fun Fudge

*So good you might get requests on birthdays for this fudge in place of cake!*

1 c. peanut butter chips
1 c. semi-sweet chocolate chips
2-1/4 c. sugar
7-oz. jar marshmallow creme

3/4 c. evaporated milk
1/4 c. butter
1-1/4 t. vanilla extract

Place peanut butter chips in a medium mixing bowl; place chocolate chips in a separate mixing bowl. Combine sugar, marshmallow creme, milk and butter in a heavy saucepan. Bring to a boil over medium heat, stirring constantly; boil and stir 5 minutes. Remove from heat and stir in vanilla. Immediately stir half of hot mixture into peanut butter chips; mix until smooth. Quickly pour into an 8"x8" pan lined with foil, with foil extending over edges of pan. Stir remaining hot mixture into chocolate chips until chips are completely melted; pour over peanut butter layer. Allow fudge to cool completely. Use foil to remove fudge from pan; invert on cutting board and peel off foil. Cut into squares. Store in an airtight container. Makes 2 pounds.

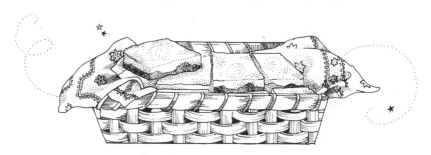

Plan a double-fun day for Dad on Fathers' Day...maybe hiking, fishing, a movie or a ball game. Write up the day's highlights and present to Dad in a homemade card.

# Raspberry Ripple Brownies

*These moist, chewy brownies won't last long...you may want to make a double batch!*

1 c. frozen raspberries, thawed, rinsed and drained
9 1-oz. sqs. white baking chocolate, chopped
3/4 c. all-purpose flour
1/2 t. salt
6 T. butter
3/4 c. sugar
3 eggs
1 t. vanilla extract
1 t. almond extract
Garnish: powdered sugar

Use the back of a spoon to press raspberries through a strainer to remove seeds. Measure 1/4 cup strained purée into a small bowl; set purée aside and save any additional for another recipe. Melt white chocolate in a double boiler, stirring until smooth; set aside to cool. Combine flour and salt in a small bowl; set aside. Cream butter and sugar together until smooth. Blend in eggs, vanilla and almond extract. Beat in melted chocolate; add flour mixture just until combined and the batter is smooth. Spread batter into a buttered 8"x8" pan; drizzle raspberry purée over top. Draw a thin metal spatula gently though purée to swirl it with batter until top is marbleized. Bake at 325 degrees for 30 minutes or until an inserted toothpick comes out with a few moist crumbs. Cool brownies in the pan on a wire rack for one hour. Dust with powdered sugar and cut into squares. Makes 12 to 16.

Looking for a quick way to package sweet treats?
Arrange Raspberry Ripple Brownies in old-fashioned berry baskets or pails.

## Chocolate-Swirl Cheesecake Brownies

*Use a pretty stencil and cocoa powder to make a design on the top of the brownies for a personalized touch.*

3/4 c. butter
4  1-oz. sqs. unsweetened
   baking chocolate
2-1/4 c. sugar, divided
4 eggs, divided

1-3/4 c. all-purpose flour
8-oz. pkg. cream cheese,
   softened
1-1/2 t. vanilla extract

Melt butter and chocolate together in a heavy saucepan over low heat, stirring until smooth; cool to room temperature. Stir in 1-3/4 cups sugar. Beat in 3 eggs; stir in flour. Spread into a greased 13"x9" baking pan. Beat together cream cheese and remaining sugar. Add vanilla and remaining egg. Pour over chocolate mixture; swirl batters with a knife. Bake at 350 degrees for 30 to 35 minutes or until inserted toothpick comes out slightly sticky. Cool completely on wire rack. Makes 15 to 18 servings.

For a fun alternative, bake Chocolate-Swirl
Cheesecake Brownies in two, 8" round pans
and cut like slices of cheesecake.

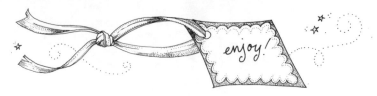

# Double Chocolate-Orange Fudge

*A blend of white and semi-sweet chocolate makes
this fudge creamy and oh-so rich!*

14-oz. can sweetened condensed
   milk, divided
8  1-oz. sqs. semi-sweet baking
   chocolate
1 t. vanilla extract

1/2 c. chopped walnuts
6  1-oz. sqs. white baking
   chocolate
2 t. orange zest

Place 3/4 cup milk in a 4-cup glass measuring cup. Add semi-sweet
chocolate and microwave on high for 3 minutes, stirring every minute
until smooth. Add vanilla and walnuts; pour into an 8"x8" pan lined
with aluminum foil. Place in refrigerator. Combine remaining milk and
white chocolate in a microwave-safe bowl. Microwave on high for
1-1/2 to 2 minutes until chocolate melts, stirring every 30 seconds.
Stir in zest and spread evenly over chocolate layer. Chill 2 hours until
firm; cut into squares. Makes 1-1/2 dozen squares.

Pair Double Chocolate-Orange Fudge with clementines in
an old-fashioned wooden crate and bring a little
sunshine to a friend in the middle of Winter.

Heavenly Sweets
from:

from the kitchen of:

OH JOY!

a little gift from ............

for ..............

to:

from:

Don't forget paper baking cups & sprinkles when giving cupcake mix.

Tie a vintage pie server onto a mix for pie crust.

perfect pie crust

you are so sweet! ♥ ♡

cakes & pies

sweet stirrings

Fill a vintage glass jar with a mix...make a gift tag from a vintage photo.

Make mini pies in a muffin tin & wrap them individually.

for you

Bake cupcakes in a new muffin tin, leave them in & tie with a bow.

# Caramel Nut Cake in a Jar

*A great gift that can be eaten on the go!*

3-1/2 c. all-purpose flour
1 t. baking powder
2 t. baking soda
2 t. salt
2 c. brown sugar, packed
1 c. butter, softened

4 eggs
2/3 c. milk
1 T. vanilla extract
1 c. chopped walnuts
6  1-pint wide-mouth canning
    jars and lids, sterilized

Sift together flour, baking powder, baking soda and salt; set aside. Cream sugar and butter together; add eggs, mixing well. Stir in milk and vanilla. Gradually add flour mixture; fold in nuts. Place one cup batter into each well-greased jar; wipe any batter from rim. Place jars on a baking sheet; bake at 325 degrees for 50 minutes or until inserted toothpick comes out clean. While jars are still hot, place lids on jars and screw on tightly; jars will seal as they cool. Place jars on a flat surface and listen for them to "ping" as they seal, or wait until they are completely cool and press on the top of the lid. If it doesn't give at all, it is sealed; cakes will last up to 6 months. Makes 6 jar cakes.

Attach a spoon and fork for a portable treat...great for road trips and family vacations!

# Cakes & Pies

## Harvest Pumpkin Tart

*A taste of Autumn that is delicious year 'round.*

1/3 c. quick-cooking oats, uncooked
1 c. gingersnaps, crushed
3 T. butter
1/4 t. cinnamon
2  8-oz. pkgs. cream cheese
1 t. vanilla extract

1/3 c. sugar
1 T. all-purpose flour
1 egg
1/4 c. plus 2 T. milk, divided
1 c. canned pumpkin
1/3 c. brown sugar, packed
1/2 t. pumpkin pie spice

In a small bowl, combine oats, gingersnaps, butter and cinnamon; mix well. Coat a 10" tart pan with a removable bottom with non-stick vegetable spray. Press oat mixture in the bottom and up the sides of the pan. Bake at 375 degrees for 6 minutes or until set; set aside. In a large bowl, combine cream cheese, vanilla, sugar, flour, egg and 2 tablespoons milk; beat until smooth and creamy. Reserve 2/3 cup cream cheese filling and set aside. In a small bowl, combine pumpkin, brown sugar, pumpkin pie spice and remaining milk; add to the remaining cream cheese batter, mixing well. Spoon into baked crust. Spoon dollops of reserved 2/3 cup cream cheese filling over pumpkin filling. Use a table knife to swirl mixtures until marbleized. Bake at 375 degrees for 25 to 30 minutes or until set. Cool 10 minutes; remove sides of pan and chill for at least one hour. Just before serving, spoon caramel sauce over tart. Serves 10.

## Caramel Sauce:

1/2 c. brown sugar, packed
1/4 c. corn syrup
2 T. water

1 T. butter
1/4 t. vanilla extract

Combine all ingredients in a small saucepan over medium heat. Bring to a boil for one minute, stirring constantly; remove from heat.

# Lemon-Poppy Seed Cake

*Try serving with a steamy pot of almond-flavored tea.*

2-1/4 c. cake flour
1-3/4 c. plus 2 T. sugar, divided
1 t. salt
1-1/2 T. lemon zest
1/4 c. plus 1 t. poppy seed

1-1/4 c. plus 1 T. butter,
  softened
5 eggs
3/4 c. lemon juice

Sift together flour, one cup plus 2 tablespoons sugar and salt. Mix in lemon zest, poppy seed and butter. Add eggs, one at a time, beating well after each addition. Pour batter into a greased and floured 9"x5" loaf pan. Bake at 350 degrees for one hour and 15 minutes or until an inserted toothpick comes out clean. Combine remaining sugar and lemon juice in a saucepan; cook over low heat, stirring until sugar is dissolved. Let cool to room temperature. After removing cake from oven, place pan on a wire rack; prick the top of the cake several times with a toothpick. Brush the top of the cake with lemon syrup. Cool cake slightly in the pan before removing to the wire rack to cool completely. Wrap cake in aluminum foil or plastic wrap and let sit for one day before serving. Makes 12 servings.

Surprise a friend with a "Tea for Two" party! Deliver a loaf of Lemon-Poppy Seed Cake wrapped up in a tea towel. Tie on a tea infuser and include several of their favorite teas too.

# Cakes & Pies

## Banana-Oat Cupcakes

*These are so moist and require no frosting...perfect for traveling!*

1/2 c. butter, softened
1/2 c. sugar
2 eggs
1 c. bananas, mashed
3/4 c. honey
1-1/2 c. all-purpose flour

1 c. quick-cooking oats,
  uncooked
1 t. baking powder
1 t. baking soda
1/2 t. salt

Cream butter and sugar; add eggs, bananas and honey, mixing well. In a separate bowl, combine remaining ingredients; stir into creamed mixture until just moistened. Fill paper-lined muffin cups 2/3 full. Bake at 350 degrees for 18 to 20 minutes. Cool in pan for 10 minutes before removing to a wire rack. Makes 1-1/2 dozen.

Keep a look-out for cake molds at yard sales and flea markets. They're great for filling with cupcakes and cookies...wrap with cellophane and top with a bow.

# 2-Kiss Cupcakes

*A chocoholic's dream...a rich chocolate cupcake filled and topped with even more chocolate.*

3/4 c. butter, softened
1-2/3 c. sugar
3 eggs
1-1/2 t. vanilla extract
2 c. all-purpose flour
2/3 c. baking cocoa

1-1/4 t. baking soda
1 t. salt
1/4 t. baking powder
1-1/3 c. water
60 milk chocolate drops

Cream butter, sugar, eggs and vanilla. In a separate bowl, combine flour, cocoa, baking soda, salt and baking powder; add alternately with water to butter mixture, beating just until combined. Fill paper-lined muffin cups 1/2 full with batter. Place a chocolate drop in center of each. Bake at 350 degrees for 20 minutes; remove to wire rack to cool. Frost. Top each cupcake with chocolate drop. Makes 30.

## Frosting:

1/4 c. margarine, melted
1/2 c. baking cocoa
1/3 c. milk

1 t. vanilla extract
3-1/2 c. powdered sugar

Beat margarine and cocoa together; add milk and vanilla, beating until smooth. Gradually beat in powdered sugar.

Fill a flower box (the kind a dozen roses comes in) with
2-Kiss Cupcakes for a special Valentine.

# Cakes & Pies

## Million Dollar Brownie Cakes

*These delicious cakes only taste like they cost a million dollars.*

1 c. all-purpose flour
1 c. sugar
1/2 t. baking soda
1/2 t. cinnamon
1/3 c. butter
1/4 c. water
3 T. baking cocoa

1/4 c. buttermilk
1 egg, beaten
1/2 t. vanilla extract
1/4 c. chopped walnuts
2  1-pint wide-mouth jars,
  sterilized

Grease each jar and line the bottoms with wax paper; set aside.
Combine flour, sugar, baking soda and cinnamon in a mixing bowl; set
aside. In a medium saucepan, combine butter, water and cocoa; heat
and stir until melted and well blended. Remove from heat. Stir in flour
mixture; add buttermilk, egg and vanilla. Stir in nuts. Pour mixture
into prepared jars; tightly cover jars with greased aluminum foil. Place
jars in a 4 to 6-quart slow cooker. Cover; cook on high for 2-1/2 to
3 hours or until cake springs back when lightly touched. Remove jars
from cooker; cool 10 minutes. Unmold cakes and remove wax paper.
Makes 2 cakes.

For a good-luck wish that can't be beat, attach a lottery ticket
to Million Dollar Brownie Cakes before giving.

# Caramel Cheesecake Pie

*When giving this scrumptious pie, be sure to include a handy pie server!*

9-inch refrigerated pie crust,
    unbaked
3/4 c. chopped pecans
12-oz. jar caramel ice cream
    topping, divided
1 c. white chocolate chips
8-oz. pkg. cream cheese,
    softened

1/3 c. sugar
1/2 c. whipping cream
3 egg whites
Garnish: frozen whipped
    topping, thawed

Fit pie crust into a 9" pie plate according to package directions; fold and crimp edges. Freeze crust for 30 minutes. Bake at 350 degrees for 6 to 8 minutes; set aside. Combine pecans and 1/2 cup caramel topping; smooth over crust and set aside. Place white chocolate chips in a small microwave-safe bowl; microwave on high for one minute, stirring after 30 seconds. In a separate bowl, beat cream cheese until creamy; gradually blend in sugar. Add whipping cream and melted chocolate until well blended. In a separate bowl, beat egg whites until stiff; fold into cream cheese mixture. Pour batter into prepared crust. Bake at 350 degrees for 35 minutes; cool on a wire rack. Cover and chill overnight. Before serving, dollop whipped topping over pie and drizzle with remaining caramel topping. Serves 6 to 8.

# Cakes & Pies

## Almond-Cherry Cake

*Because this cake needs to rest before serving, you can make it well in advance of any special occasion.*

2 c. candied cherries, halved
1/2 c. blanched, slivered
   almonds
2-1/4 c. cake flour, divided
2 t. baking powder
1/2 t. salt

1 c. butter, softened
1 c. sugar
1 t. almond extract
4 eggs
1/3 c. milk

Combine cherries, almonds and 1/2 cup flour in a bowl; mix until fruit is well coated. In a separate bowl, sift together remaining flour, baking powder and salt; set aside. Cream butter, sugar and almond extract until light and fluffy. Add eggs, one at a time, beating well after each addition. Alternately add flour mixture and milk to creamed mixture. Stir in floured fruits and nuts; spread into a greased and floured Bundt® pan. Bake at 300 degrees for 55 to 65 minutes or until inserted toothpick comes out clean. Cool in pan for 10 minutes; turn onto a wire rack to cool completely. Wrap in aluminum foil and store in a cool place for several days to allow flavors to blend. Serves 16.

Welcome a new daughter-in-law to the family with this wedding or shower gift. Gather family recipes in a book for her and include all the stories that go along with them.

# Blueberry Cobbler with Cinnamon Dumplings

*For an irresistible combination, give this dessert with a half-gallon of vanilla bean ice cream.*

21-oz. can blueberry pie filling
1 t. lemon zest
1 T. lemon juice
2 t. vanilla extract

5-ct. tube refrigerated
    cinnamon rolls
1/4 c. chopped pecans, toasted
2 T. brown sugar, packed

Combine first 4 ingredients in a lightly greased 8"x8" baking dish. Bake at 375 degrees for 10 minutes; remove from oven. Separate cinnamon rolls; set icing aside. Arrange rolls on top of fruit filling mixture; sprinkle with pecans and brown sugar. Bake at 375 degrees for 20 minutes. Drizzle with icing. Serves 4 to 5.

Spell out names on gift tags with simple letter stamps or stickers to give gifts an old-fashioned feeling. Make tags extra special with rick-rack, buttons and ribbon!

# Cakes & Pies

## Mix & Bake Cocoa Cake in a Jar

*A quick & easy gift for those last-minute occasions!*

1-1/3 c. sugar
1/2 t. salt
1 t. vanilla powder

2/3 c. baking cocoa
2 c. all-purpose flour
1-1/2 t. baking powder

Combine sugar, salt and vanilla powder; place in a one-quart, wide-mouth jar. Layer the baking cocoa on top; pack down tightly, then wipe the inside of the jar with a paper towel to remove any excess from the sides. Combine the flour and baking powder and add to the jar. Seal lid and attach a gift tag with baking instructions.

### Instructions:

Pour contents of jar into a 13"x9" baking pan; stir to combine. Add 3/4 cup oil, 2 teaspoons vinegar, and 2 cups water. Stir together using a wire whisk or fork, making certain that all ingredients are completely mixed together. Bake at 350 degrees for 35 minutes. Frost as desired or serve sprinkled with powdered sugar with fresh fruit on the side. Serves 10 to 12.

Attach a bag of mini marshmallows to a jar of Mix & Bake Cocoa Cake. Add the following to the instructions: After baking, immediately sprinkle marshmallows on top; return to oven for 5 minutes. Spread melted marshmallows over brownies.

# Sweet Pretzel Tart

*A refreshing change from ordinary cakes and tarts.*

1/2 c. butter, softened
1/2 c. sugar
1-3/4 c. pretzels, crushed
3.4-oz. pkg. instant lemon
  pudding mix

8-oz. pkg. cream cheese,
  softened
1 c. powdered sugar
12-oz. container frozen whipped
  topping, thawed

Cream together butter and sugar; mix in pretzels. Press mixture into a 13"x9" baking pan; cover and refrigerate. Prepare lemon pudding mix according to package directions. In a separate bowl, combine cream cheese and powdered sugar; blend well. Fold in whipped topping. Spread cream cheese mixture over pretzel crust; spread lemon pudding over cream cheese layer. Cover and refrigerate until pudding is set. Makes 24 servings.

# Cherry-Cream Cheese Tarts

*Let the kids share in the spirit of giving...little hands can help roll the dough!*

3-oz. pkg. cream cheese,
  softened
1/2 c. butter

1 c. all-purpose flour
21-oz. can cherry pie filling

Blend cream cheese and butter; stir in flour just until blended. Chill for one hour. Shape dough into 24 one-inch balls and press into ungreased mini muffin cups to make a shallow shell. Spoon one tablespoon pie filling into each center; bake at 325 for 20 to 25 minutes. Makes 24 tarts.

# Cakes & Pies ♡

## Creamy Black Forest Pie

*You won't believe how easy this yummy pie is to make!*

1-1/2 c. plain yogurt
1 c. milk
2  3.9 oz. pkgs. instant chocolate
    pudding mix
48 frozen, pitted cherries,
    thawed and divided

9-inch graham cracker pie crust
Garnish: frozen whipped
    topping, thawed

In a blender, process yogurt and milk until smooth; add pudding mix, blending until thick and smooth. Pour mixture into a large bowl; fold in 40 cherries. Spread mixture in pie crust; cover and refrigerate at least 4 hours or overnight. Before serving, top with whipped topping and remaining cherries. Serves 8.

Baking a homemade pie for a friend? Surprise them by
delivering it in a pretty woven pie basket, ceramic
pie plate or on an elegant stand for them to keep.
They'll love it...two gifts in one!

## Banana Split Cake

*This cake is the perfect finish to a summer picnic or cookout!*

2 c. graham cracker crumbs
3/4 c. sugar
1/2 c. butter, melted
2  8-oz. pkgs. cream cheese
1-1/2 c. powdered sugar
1/2 t. vanilla extract
4 bananas, sliced

15-oz. can crushed pineapple,
  drained
16-oz. container frozen whipped
  topping, thawed
16-oz. jar maraschino cherries,
  drained
3/4 lb. peanuts, crushed

Combine graham cracker crumbs, sugar and butter; mix well.
Press mixture into a 13"x9" pan; chill. Beat together cream cheese,
powdered sugar and vanilla; spread over chilled crust. Layer bananas
and pineapple over cream cheese mixture; cover with whipped
topping. Sprinkle cherries and nuts over cake; chill until serving.
Serves 12 to 14.

Give a Banana Split Cake along with strawberry preserves and
some hot fudge sauce for a quick summertime treat!

# Cakes & Pies

## Pineapple Upside-Down Cupcakes

*Sweet, fun cupcakes are a welcome treat at a child's birthday party.*

1/2 c. butter, divided
7 T. brown sugar, packed
1 t. cinnamon
3/4 c. pineapple tidbits, drained,
    juice reserved
6 maraschino cherries, drained
    and halved

1 c. cake flour
1-1/2 t. baking powder
1/2 t. salt
1 egg, separated
1/4 c. sugar
1 t. vanilla extract

Melt 1/4 cup butter in a small saucepan; stir in sugar and cinnamon until blended. Remove pan from heat; add pineapple. Lightly grease each cup in a 12-cup muffin tin; spoon one tablespoon mixture into each cup. Place a cherry half, round-side down, in the center of each cup; set aside. In a small bowl, combine flour, baking powder and salt. In a separate bowl, beat egg white until stiff peaks form. In a large mixing bowl, cream remaining butter and sugar; beat in egg yolk and vanilla. Alternately add flour mixture and 1/2 cup reserved pineapple juice, beating well after each addition; fold in egg white. Pour mixture evenly into muffin cups. Bake at 350 degrees for 20 to 25 minutes until cupcakes test done. Cool in pan on a wire rack for 10 minutes; invert onto a baking sheet to cool. Makes 12.

Turn a frown upside-down! Deliver a batch of Pineapple Upside-Down Cupcakes in the muffin tin tied with a cheery bow...it's sure to brighten anyone's day.

# Spiced Applesauce Cake

*Fresh-from-the-orchard taste in individual-size cakes.*

1/3 c. shortening
1-1/3 c. sugar
2 eggs
1 c. applesauce
1/3 c. water
1-2/3 c. all-purpose flour
1/4 t. baking powder
1 t. baking soda

3/4 t. salt
1/2 t. cinnamon
1/4 t. ground ginger
1/2 t. ground cloves
1/3 c. chopped walnuts
8  12-oz. wide-mouth canning
   jars and lids, sterilized

Cream together shortening and sugar; beat in eggs, one at a time, until mixture is light and fluffy. Add applesauce and water; set aside. In another bowl, sift together flour, baking powder, baking soda, salt, cinnamon, ginger and cloves; blend into applesauce mixture. Fold in nuts. Pour batter into heavily greased jars, filling them 1/2 full; place jars on a baking sheet. Bake at 325 degrees for 35 to 40 minutes or until an inserted toothpick comes out clean. Secure lids, screwing down tightly. Place jars on a flat surface and listen for them to "ping" as they seal, or wait until they are completely cool and press on the top of the lid. If it doesn't give at all, it is sealed; cakes will last up to 6 months. Makes 8 jars.

Fill a bushel basket with Spiced Applesauce Cake, a gallon of cider and fresh apples...give to a friend to help celebrate Autumn.

# Cakes & Pies

## Hummingbird Cake

*A sweet Southern tradition...versions of this recipe have won blue ribbons at county fairs across the country.*

3 c. all-purpose flour
2 c. sugar
1 t. baking soda
1 t. salt
1-1/2 c. oil

3 eggs
8-oz. can crushed pineapple, drained
2 c. bananas, mashed
1 c. chopped black walnuts

Sift together flour, sugar, baking soda and salt; set aside. In a separate bowl, combine oil, eggs, pineapple, bananas and nuts. Add flour mixture, mixing with your hands. Pour batter into 2 greased and floured 9" cake pans. Bake at 350 degrees for one hour or until cake tests done; remove from oven and allow to cool on wire racks. Evenly spread frosting on side and top of one cake; top with second cake and completely cover in frosting. Serves 10 to 12.

## Frosting:

8-oz. pkg. cream cheese, softened
1/2 c. butter, softened

16-oz. pkg. powdered sugar
1 t. vanilla extract

Blend all ingredients until smooth.

# Orange Cream Cake in a Cup

*Try different combinations...lemon cake with lemon pudding or
devil's food cake with chocolate pudding!*

18-1/2 oz. pkg. white cake mix
3.4-oz. pkg. instant vanilla
   pudding mix
16 plastic zipping bags

2-2/3 c. powdered sugar, divided
12 t. orange drink mix, divided
8  12-oz. microwave-safe
   coffee mugs

Place cake mix and pudding mix in a large bowl, blend well with a
wire whisk. Place 1/2 cup dry mix into 8 plastic zipping bags; smooth
each bag to remove as much air as possible before sealing. Label each
bag "Cake Mix." Place 1/3 cup powdered sugar and 1-1/2 teaspoons
drink mix in each remaining bag; label these bags "Glaze Mix." Place
one of each mix into each mug. Attach a gift tag with instructions to
cups. Makes 8.

## Instructions:

Generously coat inside of mug with non-stick vegetable spray. Empty
Cake Mix into mug. Add one egg white, one tablespoon oil and one
tablespoon water; stir well until combined. Microwave on high for
2 minutes. While cake is cooking, place Glaze Mix into a small bowl;
add 1-1/2 teaspoons water and mix well. Pour glaze over warm cake.

College kids missing
Mom's fresh-baked
goodies? Send an
Orange Cream Cake
in a Cup to
students living
away from home.

# Cakes & Pies

## Peanut Butter-Filled Chocolate Cupcakes

*These cupcakes are so decadent, it's hard to eat just one!*

1 c. all-purpose flour
1 c. brown sugar, packed
1/3 c. baking cocoa
3/4 t. baking soda
1/4 t. salt

1/4 c. margarine, softened
1/3 c. milk
2 egg whites, whipped

Combine flour, brown sugar, cocoa, baking soda and salt in a mixing bowl; set aside. Combine remaining ingredients in a separate mixing bowl. Mix in dry ingredients just until moistened. Grease and flour 12 muffin cups; place 2 tablespoons batter into each cup. Spoon a rounded teaspoonful of filling into center of each. Fill cups 1/2 full with remaining batter, one tablespoon each. Bake at 375 degrees for 20 minutes. Makes 12.

### Filling:

4 oz. cream cheese, softened
1/4 c. creamy peanut butter
1 T. honey

1 T. milk
2 T. vanilla extract

Blend together all ingredients.

After removing Peanut Butter-Filled Chocolate Cupcakes from
the oven, immediately place a peanut butter cup
on top, upside-down, and allow to melt.
Deliver them with a gallon of cold milk!

# Carnival Funnel Cake Mix

*For a fruity funnel cake, serve with cherry or blueberry pie filling.*

1-2/3 c. all-purpose flour
1/4 t. salt
3/4 t. baking soda

1/2 t. cream of tartar
2 T. sugar

Combine all ingredients; place in a plastic zipping bag and attach instructions.

## Instructions:

In a mixing bowl, beat together one egg and one cup milk. Beat in funnel cake mix until smooth. Heat one inch oil in frying pan to 375 degrees. Pour batter, 1/2 cup at a time, through a funnel into oil with a circular motion to form a spiral. Fry until golden; turn to fry each side. Remove to drain on paper towels. Repeat with remaining batter. Sprinkle with powdered sugar while warm. Makes 5 to 8 cakes.

Clever! Place a bag of Carnival Funnel Cake Mix in a funnel before giving...add a shaker of powdered sugar too.

# Cakes & Pies

## Picnic-Perfect Cupcakes

*Look for decorative paper cupcake liners to match holidays, birthdays and other special occasions.*

18-1/2 oz. pkg. chocolate
   cake mix
8-oz. pkg. cream cheese,
   softened

1 egg, lightly beaten
1/3 c. sugar
6-oz. pkg. semi-sweet chocolate
   chips

Prepare cake mix according to package directions; spoon batter into 24 paper-lined muffin cups, filling each 2/3 full. In a mixing bowl, mix cream cheese, egg and sugar until smooth; fold in chocolate chips. Drop by tablespoonfuls into batter. Bake at 350 degrees for 20 minutes or until cupcakes test done. Makes 24.

Try baking Picnic-Perfect Cupcakes in ice cream cones. Just fill the cones with batter to 1/2 inch from the top and place on a baking sheet before baking. Great for taking to the park or on school trips.

# Top Secret Pie Crust

*A simple recipe for a light, flaky crust.*

4 T. butter
5 T. shortening
3/4 c. cake flour
3/4 c. all-purpose flour
1 t. sugar
1 t. salt

1/8 t. baking powder
1 egg yolk
2 t. white vinegar
3 ice cubes
1/2 c. cold water

Place butter and shortening onto a plate and put into freezer for
20 minutes. Combine flours, sugar, salt and baking powder in a food
processor; pulse for a few seconds to mix. Add half cold butter and
half cold shortening; pulse for one minute. Add remaining butter and
shortening; cut in very briefly with processor, leaving pea-size crumbs.
In a small bowl, mix together egg yolk and vinegar; add ice cubes and
water. Allow to sit for 3 to 4 minutes. Place flour and shortening mix
into a large mixing bowl; sprinkle with 4 to 5 tablespoons of vinegar
mixture, mixing gently with a fork. Place dough into plastic wrap; chill
for 5 minutes. Remove from refrigerator and roll out. Makes one crust.

To give Top Secret Pie Crust as a gift, combine flours, sugar,
salt and baking powder in a plastic zipping bag. Place bag
along with a copy of the recipe into an old-fashioned
recipe box...add a "Top Secret" label to the front.

# Cakes & Pies

## Double Raspberry Pie

*Right before serving, garnish with fresh whipped cream.*

1 c. all-purpose flour
1/2 c. butter
2 T. powdered sugar

4 c. fresh raspberries
8-oz. jar raspberry jam

Blend together flour, butter and sugar; chill for one hour. Pat mixture into a 9" tart pan; bake at 375 degrees for 10 minutes. Remove from oven and cool. Arrange raspberries in cooled crust. Heat jam in microwave until boiling; pour over fruit. Cover and refrigerate for one hour. Serves 6 to 8.

## No-Bake Pineapple Pie

*This pie is so quick & easy to make...plus, you make it
the night before!*

14-oz. can sweetened condensed
  milk
1/4 c. lemon juice
1/3 c. chopped maraschino
  cherries
1 t. vanilla extract

1/3 c. chopped pecans
8-oz. can crushed pineapple,
  drained
9-inch graham cracker pie crust
Garnish: frozen whipped
  topping, thawed

Combine milk and lemon juice; stir until blended. Stir in cherries, vanilla, pecans and pineapple; spoon into pie crust. Chill 8 hours or overnight. Top with whipped topping before serving. Serves 6 to 8.

# Apple-Cinnamon Cobbler

*You're guaranteed smiles at any party when you bring along this
sweet and nutty cobbler.*

4-1/3 c. apples, thinly sliced
1-1/2 c. sugar, divided
1/2 t. cinnamon
3/4 c. chopped pecans, divided
1 c. all-purpose flour

1 t. baking powder
1/2 t. salt
1 egg, beaten
1/2 c. evaporated milk
1/3 c. butter, melted

Arrange apple slices in an even layer in a generously greased 2-quart
baking dish. In a small bowl, combine 1/2 cup sugar, cinnamon and
1/2 cup pecans; sprinkle mixture over apples. In a separate bowl,
combine flour, remaining sugar, baking powder and salt; set aside. In a
small bowl, whisk together egg, milk and butter; add to flour mixture
all at once, stirring until smooth. Pour mixture over apples; sprinkle
top with remaining pecans. Bake at 325 degrees for 55 minutes.
Serves 8.

So thoughtful for newlyweds...purchase a new baking dish,
fill it with homemade Apple-Cinnamon Cobbler and deliver
with the recipe. They can keep the dish!

# Cakes & Pies

## Zucchini Cake in a Jar

*A perfect gift for a family...everyone gets their own cake!*

3 c. all-purpose flour
2 t. salt
1 t. baking soda
1 t. baking powder
2 t. cinnamon
1/4 t. nutmeg
1/4 t. ground cloves

3 eggs, beaten
2 c. sugar
1 c. margarine, softened
2 c. zucchini, grated
1 t. vanilla extract
6  1-pint wide-mouth canning
   jars and lids, sterilized

Combine flour, salt, baking soda, baking powder, cinnamon, nutmeg and cloves; set aside. In a separate mixing bowl, combine eggs, sugar, margarine, zucchini and vanilla; mix in dry ingredients. Pour batter equally into heavily greased jars. Wipe jar rims; place jars on a baking sheet. Bake at 325 degrees for 40 minutes; immediately secure lids, tightening in place. Place jars on a wire rack to cool; check for seal. Makes 6 jars.

To dress up jars, cut out a circle of decorative fabric 2 inches larger in diameter than the jar lid. Place fabric over lid and secure with ribbon or jute. Add buttons, rick-rack or an old-fashioned mailing tag...how charming!

# Sweetheart Red Velvet Cake

*Try topping with rich cream cheese frosting...mmmm!*

18-1/2 oz. pkg. white cake mix      red food coloring, as desired
1/2 c. buttermilk
3.4-oz. pkg. cook & serve
   chocolate pudding mix

Prepare cake mix according to package directions, substituting half of the water called for with buttermilk. Stir in pudding mix and food coloring. Pour into a greased 13"x9" baking pan and bake according to package directions. Makes 12 to 15 servings.

Divide Sweetheart Red Velvet Cake batter between an
8" round pan and 8"x8" pan before baking. Once cooled, slice
round cake in half and place each piece on 2 adjacent
sides of the square to make a heart!

# MY FAVORITE Dessert

MIX

in the whole, wide wonderful world!

from: ............................

Feel free to copy these tags and use colored pens to give them more ...ZING!

for

from:

to:

from:

How about a little glitter on the cherries?

Don't forget to include your instructions on the back side!

OH MY, Homemade Pie

a little gift from:

· · · · · · · · · ·

for:

· · · · · · · · · ·

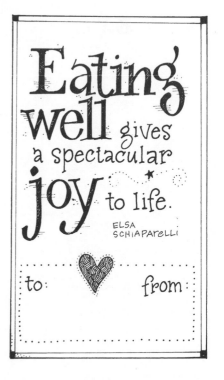

Eating well gives a spectacular joy to life.

ELSA SCHIAPARELLI

to: from:

Tuck your soup mix into a big measuring cup along with a wooden spoon & tea towel.

When you give a pot of soup, don't forget a stack of bowls tied with a ribbon.

Tie on a new ladle to a jar of soup.

Soups
AND
More

Cut out crispy croutons with mini cookie cutters.

Set a soup mix inside a stockpot with some crunchy crackers.

CRACKER

A chunk of fresh cheese, a grater and chili mix...

# Warm-'Em-Up Alphabet Soup

*A fun soup for kids just learning their ABC's!*

1/2 c. pearled barley
1/2 c. dried split peas
1/2 c. instant rice, uncooked
1/2 c. dried lentils
2 T. dried, minced onion
2 T. dried parsley

2-1/2 t. salt
1/2 t. lemon pepper
2 T. beef bouillon granules
1/2 c. alphabet pasta, uncooked
1 c. rotini, uncooked

In a one-quart, wide-mouth jar, layer barley, peas, rice and lentils.
Pour in onion, parsley, salt, lemon pepper, bouillon and alphabet
pasta; fill remaining space with rotini. Seal lid and attach instructions.

## Instructions:

Combine jar contents with 3 quarts water in a large pot. Add 2 stalks
chopped celery, 2 sliced carrots, one cup shredded cabbage and 2 cups
diced tomatoes. Cover; heat over medium-low for one hour until
vegetables are tender. Serves 4.

Spell out a name on the gift tag using
alphabet pasta. Just glue in place and tie to
a jar of Warm-'Em-Up Alphabet Soup.

# Soups & More

## Crispy Wheat Crackers

*So delicious in soups and stews...terrific topped with cheese too!*

| | |
|---|---|
| 1-3/4 c. whole-wheat flour | 1/3 c. oil |
| 1-1/2 c. all-purpose flour | 1 c. water |
| 1 t. salt | coarse salt to taste |

In a medium mixing bowl, combine first 3 ingredients. Add oil and water, mixing until just blended. Roll dough out on a lightly floured surface to a thickness no greater than 1/8 inch. Place dough on an ungreased baking sheet; score squares with a knife without cutting through. Prick each square with a fork several times and sprinkle with salt. Bake at 350 degrees for 15 to 20 minutes until crisp and golden. Allow crackers to cool on baking sheet. Remove and break into individual crackers. Makes 32 servings.

Pack a batch of Crispy Wheat Crackers along with a favorite soup mix in a ceramic soup bowl...great for a loved one feeling under the weather.

# Texas Two-Step in a Jar

*This yummy mix will have 'em dancing in the streets!*

1.6-oz. pkg. brown gravy mix
2 T. mild chili powder
2 t. dried oregano
1 t. cumin
1 t. dried, minced onion

1 t. garlic salt
10 to 12 tortilla chips, coarsely
   crushed
1-1/4 c. pasta wheels, uncooked

Pour gravy mix into a one-pint, wide-mouth jar. In a small bowl, combine chili powder, oregano, cumin, onion and garlic salt; pour on top of gravy mix. Add tortilla chips and pasta to fill jar; secure lid. Tie on a gift tag with instructions.

## Instructions:

Brown 1/2 pound ground beef in a large saucepan. Add jar contents and 7 cups of water; bring to a boil. Stir in 15-ounce can corn and 16-ounce can chopped tomatoes. Reduce heat, cover and simmer for 20 to 25 minutes until pasta is tender. Garnish with tortilla chips and shredded Monterey Jack cheese. Serves 8.

For an anniversary gift that'll have them kicking up their heels, give Texas Two-Step in a Jar along with a gift certificate for dancing lessons.

# Soups & More

## Fiesta Rice Mix

*Add a little spice to a hostess gift by including this tasty rice mix.*

4 c. instant long-grain rice,
  uncooked
3 t. salt
1 t. dried basil

1/2 c. dried green pepper flakes
5 t. dried parsley
1 t. cumin

Combine all ingredients in a large bowl; stir until well blended. Place 1-1/2 cups of mix into 3 airtight containers or plastic zipping bags. Give each with cooking instructions.

### Instructions:

Bring 2 cups water and one tablespoon butter to a boil in a medium saucepan; reduce heat. Stir in rice mix, reduce heat and cover. Cook until liquid is absorbed, about 15 to 20 minutes. Makes 4 to 6 servings.

Add a bag of homemade tortilla chips to this mix. Simply cut flour or corn tortillas into quarters and fry in oil until crispy. Season with salt and chili pepper, if desired...so easy!

# Turkey Noodle Soup in a Jar

*Make several batches to keep on hand for last-minute gifts during the holiday season.*

1/4 c. dried red lentils
2 T. dried, minced onion
1 T. plus 1-1/2 t. chicken
    bouillon granules
1/2 t. dill weed

1/8 t. celery seed
1/8 t. salt
1/8 t. garlic powder
1 bay leaf
1 c. egg noodles, uncooked

In a one-pint, wide-mouth jar, layer ingredients in the order listed. Seal jar and attach cooking instructions.

## Instructions:

Bring 8 cups water to a boil in a large saucepan; stir in jar contents. Cover, reduce heat and simmer 15 minutes. Remove and discard bay leaf. Stir in a 10-ounce package frozen mixed vegetables and 2 cups cooked and diced turkey. Cook 5 minutes until meat and vegetables are tender. Makes 10 cups.

Give Turkey Noodle Soup in a Jar to the hostess
of Thanksgiving dinner...it's a quick meal
to make with leftover turkey!

# Soups & More

## Creamy Potato Soup Mix

*A great way to snuggle in on a chilly day.*

1-3/4 c. instant mashed potatoes
1-1/2 c. powdered milk
2 T. chicken bullion granules
2 t. dried, minced onion
1 t. dried parsley

1/4 t. white pepper
1/4 t. dried thyme
1/8 t. turmeric
2 t. seasoned salt

Combine all ingredients in a large mixing bowl. Place in a one-quart, wide-mouth jar; seal lid. Attach instructions to jar.

### Instructions:

Place 1/2 cup soup mix in a bowl; add one cup boiling water. Stir until smooth. Makes one serving.

Attach an old-fashioned scoop to a jar of Creamy Potato
Soup Mix for quick & easy measuring.

# Hearty Soup Mix in a Jar

*Perfect for even the biggest appetites!*

1/2 c. dried split peas
1/3 c. beef bouillon granules
1/4 c. pearled barley
1/2 c. dried lentils
1/4 c. dried, minced onion
2 t. Italian seasoning

1/2 t. celery salt
1/2 c. instant long-grain rice,
   uncooked
2 bay leaves
1/2 c. rigatoni, uncooked

In a 1-1/2 pint, wide-mouth jar, layer peas, bouillon, barley, lentils, onion, seasoning, celery salt, rice and bay leaves. Wrap pasta in plastic wrap and place in jar; seal tightly. Attach instructions.

## Instructions:

Remove pasta from jar and set aside. In a large pot over medium heat, brown one pound ground beef with pepper and garlic to taste; drain. Add 28-ounce can diced tomatoes, 6-ounce can tomato paste, 3 quarts water and jar contents. Bring to a boil. Reduce heat to low, cover and simmer 45 minutes. Add pasta, cover and simmer 15 to 20 minutes until tender. Serves 16.

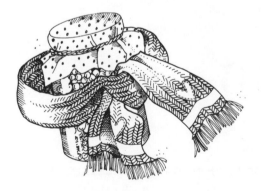

Give a jar of Hearty
Soup Mix to a
friend on the first
snowfall...wrap it
up in a warm scarf
or a pair of
fuzzy earmuffs!

# Soups & More

## Seasoned Rice Mix

*Cut out pictures from empty seed packets to use as gift tags...so charming.*

3 lbs. instant long-grain rice
2 c. dried celery flakes
2/3 c. dried, minced onion
1/2 c. dried parsley
2 T. dried chives
1 T. dried tarragon

1 T. dried oregano
3 t. salt
2 t. pepper
5 1-pint, wide-mouth jars
 and lids

Combine all ingredients; mix well. Place two cups in each jar and secure lids. Attach instructions to each. Makes 5 jars.

## Instructions:

In a saucepan over medium heat, bring 2-2/3 cup water and 1/4 cup butter to a boil; add one cup mixture. Reduce heat; cover and simmer for 20 minutes. Remove from heat; let stand for 5 minutes or until liquid is absorbed. Fluff with a fork. Makes 4 servings.

Give a personal herb garden! Choose a narrow wooden
crate that will fit on a windowsill. Fill it with starter
pots of herbs...rosemary, basil, oregano and
thyme make a yummy kitchen sampler.

# Patchwork Soup Mix

*This hearty soup is a great chill chaser.*

1/3 c. dried yellow split peas
1/3 c. dried green split peas
1/3 c. dried lima beans
1/3 c. dried pinto beans
1/3 c. dried kidney beans
1/3 c. dried Great
    Northern beans

1/4 c. dried, minced onion
3 t. chicken bouillon granules
1/4 t. cumin
1/4 t. garlic powder
1/8 t. dried oregano

Combine all ingredients in an airtight container. Attach a gift tag with cooking instructions.

## Instructions:

Combine 8 cups water and soup mix in a large pot; bring to a boil. Cover, remove from heat and let sit one hour. Return pot to heat, stir in 2 chopped carrots and 2 chopped celery stalks. Add 2 pounds smoked ham hocks; bring to a boil. Cover, reduce heat and simmer 2 hours until beans are tender; skim fat as necessary. Remove ham hocks from soup; remove meat from bone, chop and return to soup. Heat through and serve. Serves 10.

# Soups & More

## Herbed Oyster Crackers

*Pair with a yummy soup mix for a tummy-pleasing gift.*

2  10-oz. pkgs. oyster crackers
1 c. oil
1-1/2 T. ranch dressing mix

1 t. lemon pepper
1 t. dill weed
1 t. garlic salt

Toss crackers and oil until completely coated. Add remaining ingredients, mixing well. Spread in a single layer on an ungreased baking sheet; bake at 250 degrees for 10 minutes. Store in an airtight container. Makes 24 servings.

## Cheese & Garlic Croutons

*These savory croutons are delicious sprinkled in a bowl of soup or tossed in a dinner salad.*

4 T. butter
1/2 t. dried oregano
1/2 t. dried basil
1/2 t. celery salt

2 cloves garlic, minced
1 T. onion, minced
2 c. whole-wheat bread, cubed
2 T. Parmesan cheese, grated

Heat butter in a large skillet. Add seasonings, garlic and onion; cook for about one minute to soften. Stir in bread cubes; saute until browned and crisp. Toss with cheese until evenly distributed. Croutons may be reheated and crisped in a 350-degree oven for 5 minutes. Makes 4 servings.

# Split Pea Soup Mix

*This flavorful soup can be cooked with or without meat.*

2-1/2 c. dried green split peas
2-1/2 c. dried lentils
2-1/2 c. pearled barley
2 c. macaroni, uncooked
1 c. dried, minced onion

1/2 c. dried celery flakes
1/2 c. dried parsley
1-1/2 t. dried thyme
1-1/2 t. white pepper

Mix all ingredients together. Store in an airtight container. Attach cooking instructions for giving.

## Instructions:

Combine one cup soup mix with 4 cups water in a large pot. Add one cup chopped chicken, if desired. Bring to a boil; reduce heat to low, cover pan and simmer for 45 to 60 minutes or until peas are tender. Serves 4.

Add some crunchy crouton sticks to this soup mix...they're perfect for dunking. Just cut bread into strips, brush with butter and sprinkle on herbs. Bake at 300 degrees until they're crispy!

# Soups & More

## Celebration Bean Soup

*It's a party in every jar!*

12 1-pint, wide-mouth jars
   and lids
2 lbs. dried baby lima beans
2 lbs. dried lentils
2 lbs. dried red lentils
2 lbs. dried black-eyed peas
2 lbs. dried pinto beans

2 lbs. dried white beans
2 lbs. dried navy beans
2 lbs. dried kidney beans
12 cubes Italian-flavored
   bouillon
12 bay leaves

In each jar, layer 1/4 cup of each type of bean. Place one bouillon cube and one bay leaf on top of the beans in each jar. Seal lid and attach cooking instructions. Makes 12 jars.

### Instructions:

Set aside bouillon cube and bay leaf. Rinse beans and place in a large pot. Add 6 to 8 cups hot water; bring to a rapid boil and boil 2 minutes; remove from heat. Cover and let stand one hour. Drain water and rinse beans. Add 6 cups water, 14-ounce can chopped tomatoes, bay leaf and bouillon cube. Simmer over medium-low heat until beans are tender, about 2 hours. Season with salt and pepper to taste. Makes 4 servings.

Top a jar of Celebration Bean Soup mix with a party hat...a fun and welcome hostess gift.

# Wild Rice & Mushroom Soup Mix

*A warm & cozy way to say "thanks."*

2-3/4-oz. pkg. country gravy
   mix
1-1/2 T. chicken bouillon
   granules
2 t. dried, minced onion
2 t. dried celery flakes

1 t. dried parsley
1/4 c. instant wild rice,
   uncooked
1 c. instant rice, uncooked
2 T. dried mushrooms, chopped

Pour gravy mix into a one-pint, wide-mouth jar. Combine bouillon granules, onion, celery and parsley in a small bowl; pour over gravy mix. Layer on rice and mushrooms; seal lid. Attach a tag with instructions.

## Instructions:

Empty jar into a large saucepan. Add 7 cups water; bring to a boil. Reduce heat, cover and simmer 25 to 30 minutes, stirring occasionally, until rice is tender. Serves 6.

Present a soup mix in a pretty fabric bag! Just cut a square dinner napkin in half to form 2 rectangles. Fold right sides of one piece together so the fold forms the bottom of the bag. Stitch sides, leaving top open. Turn right-side out, place mix inside and tie with raffia.

# Soups & More

## Homestyle Chicken Soup in a Jar

*This good-for-you soup is chock-full of flavor!*

1/3 c. chicken bouillon granules
1/4 c. dried, minced onion
1/2 c. shell macaroni, uncooked
2/3 c. pearled barley, uncooked
1/2 c. spinach pasta, uncooked
and broken into small pieces

1/3 c. long-cooking long-grain
rice, uncooked
1 T. garlic powder
1 t. pepper
1 t. dried oregano

In a one-quart, wide-mouth jar layer bouillon, onion, macaroni, barley, spinach pasta and rice. Combine remaining ingredients in a small plastic bag and place on top of layers. Seal lid and attach instructions.

## Instructions:

Pour all jar contents into a large pot filled with 12 cups water; bring to a boil. Reduce heat and simmer for 45 minutes. Add one cup cooked, cubed chicken; simmer 15 minutes. Serves 4 to 6.

Cheer up an under-the-weather friend! Fill a fabric-lined basket with Homestyle Chicken Soup in a Jar, some hearty crackers, a big mug and a cheerful book to read while recovering.

# Lemon-Dill Rice Mix

*They're sure to ask for the recipe...it's up to you whether or not to keep it a secret!*

4 c. instant long-grain rice, uncooked
1/4 c. chicken bouillon granules
2 T. dill weed

1 T. dried chives
1/4 c. dried lemon zest
1 t. salt

Combine all ingredients in a large bowl and stir until evenly distributed. Place in an airtight container and attach instructions.

## Instructions:

Bring 2 cups water and one tablespoon butter to a simmer in a medium saucepan. Stir in one cup rice mix; reduce heat and cover. Cook until liquid is absorbed, about 15 to 20 minutes. Makes about 4 servings.

Place Lemon-Dill Rice Mix in a cellophane bag, fold the top over and staple. Fold a piece of colored paper over the top...make the front a gift tag and put cooking instructions on the back.

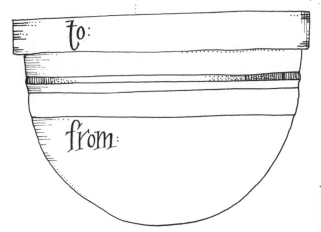

to:

from:

Make a copy
of these little
tags and tie
them on for
extra·special gifts.

brrr...

from the kitchen of:

# Eat Soup

first & eat it last and live 'til a hundred years be past.

OLD FRENCH PROVERB

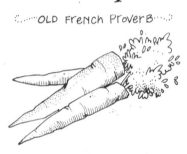

eat your vegetables

Include the pan when giving mini loaves

Cut out pats of mini butter using mini cookie cutters.

Attach a set of spreaders to your gift.

Muffins & Breads

Give your freshly baked loaf on a bread board.

Mini muffins are especially sweet when delivered in a vintage lunchbox.

Yummy!

Use a basket to give your mini loaves or muffins.

## Quick & Easy Pancake Mix

*Sprinkle fresh blueberries and strawberries on top of these moist,
golden pancakes...so tasty!*

10 c. all-purpose flour
2-1/2 c. powdered milk
1/2 c. sugar

1/4 c. baking powder
1-1/2 T. salt

Combine all ingredients; blend well. Place in a large container or divide
by 2-cup amounts into plastic zipping bags. Store in a cool, dry place
for up to 8 months. Attach instructions. Makes 12 cups.

## Instructions:

Combine 2 cups mix, one beaten egg and 1-1/4 cup water or milk
until just moistened; drop by 1/4 cupfuls onto a hot, greased griddle or
skillet. Turn when bubbles form on the surface; heat until golden.
Makes 12 to 14 pancakes.

Good morning! Pair up Quick & Easy Pancake Mix with jars of
fruit-flavored syrups for a yummy breakfast-time gift.

# Muffins & Breads

## Maple Twisties

*Perfect for Sunday brunch!*

3-oz. pkg. cream cheese,
   softened
1/4 c. powdered sugar
2 T. margarine, softened
1 c. brown sugar, packed
1/2 c. chopped walnuts

1/3 c. maple syrup
2 c. biscuit baking mix
1/4 c. milk
2 T. sugar
1 egg, beaten
1 t. cinnamon

Blend cream cheese, powdered sugar and margarine together until light and fluffy; set aside. Mix brown sugar, walnuts and syrup together; spread mixture evenly in a 13"x9" ungreased baking pan. Combine remaining ingredients in another mixing bowl; beat vigorously 20 strokes. Knead 8 times on a surface lightly dusted with baking mix. Roll dough out into a 16"x9" rectangle; spread with cream cheese mixture. Fold the dough lengthwise into thirds; press edges to seal. Cut into 16, one-inch strips; gently twist ends in opposite directions one full twist. Arrange on top of brown sugar mixture in baking dish. Bake at 425 degrees for 15 minutes; serve warm. Makes 16.

Neighbors heading off for vacation? Deliver a dish of Maple Twisties with a thermos of piping hot coffee...they'll start the trip on the right foot!

# Basic Buttermilk Baking Mix

*This versatile baking mix is a must-have in the pantry.*

10-1/2 c. all-purpose flour
1/4 c. baking powder
1-1/2 T. salt
1/2 c. sugar

2 c. shortening
1 c. buttermilk powder
1-1/2 t. baking soda
2 t. cinnamon

Mix all the ingredients together in a large bowl until it resembles coarse crumbs. Store in an airtight container for up to 3 months. Attach instructions for Buttermilk Pancakes and Buttermilk Biscuits. Makes 13 cups mix.

## Buttermilk Pancakes:

Blend 2 cups mix, 1-2/3 cups milk and one egg until smooth; pour batter by 1/4 cupfuls onto a greased, hot griddle or skillet. Wait for bubbles to form, flip and heat until golden. Makes 18.

## Buttermilk Biscuits:

Combine 2 cups mix and 2/3 cups milk until a soft dough forms; stir 15 strokes. Knead dough 8 to 10 times until smooth; roll out to 1/2-inch thickness. Cut with floured biscuit cutter or drinking glass; bake on greased baking sheets at 450 degrees for 10 to 15 minutes. Makes 12.

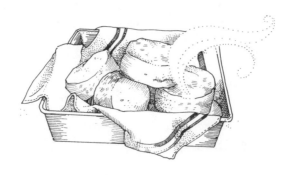

# Muffins & Breads

## Gingerbread Mix

*Delicious drizzled with warm caramel sauce.*

1 c. buttermilk biscuit
   baking mix
2 T. sugar

1/4 t. ground ginger
1/4 t. ground cloves
1/2 t. cinnamon

Combine ingredients; store in an airtight container. Attach instructions. Makes about 1-1/2 cups mix.

## Instructions:

Pour mix in large mixing bowl; set aside. Combine 1/4 cup water, 1/4 cup molasses and one egg yolk in a separate bowl; stir half of this mixture into biscuit mixture, blending for 2 minutes. Add remainder of molasses mixture; blend one more minute. Pour into a 6"x4" greased and floured loaf pan; bake at 350 degrees for 40 minutes. Top with whipped topping and bananas before serving. Makes 6 servings.

Place a jar of Gingerbread Mix in a loaf pan and add one or two bananas and caramel sauce for topping...an oh-so easy holiday treat!

## Honey-Raisin Sticky Buns

*Raisins, pecans and a drizzle of honey make these buns an
irresistible anytime-treat.*

2 pkgs. instant dry yeast
1/3 c. sugar
1 t. salt
1/4 c. milk
1/2 c. buttermilk
1 T. orange juice
1/2 t. orange zest
2 t. vanilla extract
2 egg yolks

3 c. all-purpose flour, divided
1 c. butter, softened
4 t. cinnamon
1 c. raisins
2 c. brown sugar, packed
   and divided
1/2 c. honey
1 c. chopped pecans
1/4 c. butter, melted

Combine yeast, sugar and salt; blend in next 5 ingredients until
smooth. Stir in egg yolks and 1-1/2 cups flour; blend in softened
butter and remaining flour. Knead dough on a lightly floured surface
about 10 minutes; place in a greased bowl, turning once. Cover and
refrigerate for 2 hours. Knead dough again on a lightly floured surface;
roll out into an 18"x10" rectangle; sprinkle with cinnamon, raisins and
one cup brown sugar. Roll dough jelly-roll style; slice into 3/4-inch
slices. In a small bowl, mix remaining brown sugar, honey and pecans
together; place one tablespoon mixture into 24 greased, large muffin
tins. Arrange one slice of dough on top of each pecan mixture; brush
with melted butter. Bake at 350 degrees until golden, about 35 to
40 minutes; invert onto wax paper and cool completely. Store in an
airtight container. Makes 24.

Place these sticky buns in individual wax paper bags...give to a
friend with a new job for breakfast on the go.

# Muffins & Breads

## Brown Sugar-Oatmeal Muffin Mix

*Makes enough for three batches!*

3 c. all-purpose flour
1 c. brown sugar, packed
1/2 c. sugar
3-1/2 t. baking powder

1-1/4 t. salt
1-1/2 c. shortening
3 c. quick-cooking oats,
    uncooked

Combine flour, sugars, baking powder and salt in a large mixing bowl; mix well. Cut in shortening until mixture resembles coarse crumbs; stir in oats. Store in an airtight container for up to 6 months. Attach instructions. Makes 9 cups mix.

### Instructions:

Combine 3 cups mix, one beaten egg and 2/3 cup milk; mix well. Fill paper-lined muffin cups 2/3 full; bake at 400 degrees for 15 to 20 minutes. Cool 5 minutes before removing from pan. Makes 12.

Don't throw out those plain paper bags! Just add a colorful piece of tissue paper, a vintage postcard and a ribbon bow for a charming gift bag.

# Sweet Cranberry Bread

*You won't be able to resist the aroma of this bread baking in the oven...be sure to make an extra loaf to keep for yourself!*

1 c. all-purpose flour
1 c. graham cracker crumbs
1/2 c. brown sugar, packed
2 t. baking powder
1/2 t. salt
1 c. cranberries, chopped

1 c. raisins
1/2 c. chopped walnuts
2-1/2 t. orange zest
1 egg, beaten
1 c. orange juice
1/3 c. oil

Combine flour, crumbs, brown sugar, baking powder and salt; stir in cranberries, raisins, nuts and orange zest. Add egg, orange juice and oil; stir until blended. Spread in a greased 9"x5" loaf pan; bake at 350 degrees for one hour or until a toothpick inserted in the center removes clean. Cool in pan for 10 minutes; remove loaf from pan and cool on a wire rack. Makes 8 servings.

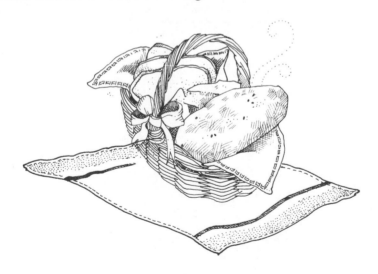

Bake Sweet Cranberry Bread in mini loaves for several gifts.
Wrap individually in colored cellophane, tea towels or just tie
a ribbon around the loaf pan!

# Muffins & Breads

## Morning O.J. Muffins

*Rise & shine!*

1/2 c. shortening
1-1/4 c. orange sugar, divided
2 eggs
2 c. all-purpose flour

1-1/4 t. baking soda
1 c. buttermilk
1/2 c. golden raisins
1/3 c. orange juice

Cream shortening with one cup orange sugar until smooth; blend in eggs until fluffy. In another mixing bowl, mix flour and baking soda together; add to creamed mixture. Blend in buttermilk; fold in raisins. Fill greased and floured muffin pans 2/3 full; bake at 350 degrees for 15 to 18 minutes. Brush with orange juice; sprinkle with remaining orange sugar. Store in an airtight container. Makes about 1-1/2 dozen.

## Orange Sugar

*Give a jar with a batch of Morning O.J. Muffins...yum!*

2/3 c. orange zest
4 cups sugar

1-1/2 t. cinnamon
1/8 t. ground cloves

Place ingredients in a blender; blend until fine. Makes about 4-1/2 cups.

## Vanilla-Pecan Quick Bread

*Great for bake sales!*

1-1/2 c. butter, divided
2-1/3 c. sugar, divided
1-1/2 c. vanilla wafers, crushed
1 c. chopped pecans
4 eggs

1 c. milk
2 t. vanilla extract
2-2/3 c. all-purpose flour
1-1/2 t. baking powder
3/4 t. salt

Melt 1/2 cup butter; mix in 1/3 cup sugar, vanilla wafer crumbs and pecans. Press mixture into the bottom of 2 greased 8"x4" loaf pans; set aside. Cream remaining butter and sugar; add eggs, one at a time, blending well after each addition; set aside. In a separate bowl, combine milk and vanilla; set aside. Combine remaining ingredients in a separate bowl; add to creamed mixture alternately with milk mixture. Mix well; pour equally into the 2 pans. Bake at 350 degrees for one hour or until a toothpick inserted in the center removes clean; cool on a wire rack. Makes 2 loaves.

*Copy & attach!*

# Muffins & Breads

### Friendship Scone Mix

*Substitute 1/2 cup sweetened, dried cranberries or 1/2 teaspoon orange zest in place of the mini chocolate chips for variety.*

1-3/4 c. all-purpose flour
1 T. baking powder
1/2 t. salt
1 c. quick-cooking oats,
    uncooked

1/2 c. chopped walnuts
1/3 c. mini semi-sweet chocolate
    chips

Combine first 3 ingredients together in a large mixing bowl; stir in remaining ingredients. Mix well. Store in an airtight container in a cool, dry place. Attach instructions. Makes 3-1/2 cups mix.

### Instructions:

Place scone mixture in a large mixing bowl; cut in 1/2 cup butter until mixture resembles coarse crumbs. In a separate bowl, whisk together 1/4 cup milk with one egg; add to crumb mixture until just moistened. Knead gently on a lightly floured surface 8 to 10 times; pat dough into an 8-inch circle. Cut into 8 wedges; place on a lightly greased baking sheet. Bake at 375 degrees until golden, about 10 to 12 minutes. Serve warm. Makes 8.

Arrange Friendship Scone Mix, packages of tea and coffee and small jars of jam and honey on a serving tray...just right for a housewarming gift.

# Spicy Pumpkin Bread in a Jar

*Don't forget the whipped cream!*

1 c. raisins
2 c. all-purpose flour
2 t. baking soda
1/4 t. baking powder
1/2 t. salt
2 t. ground cloves
2-1/2 t. cinnamon

1 t. ground ginger
4 eggs, beaten
2 c. sugar
1 c. margarine, softened
2 c. canned pumpkin
8  1-pint wide-mouth canning
   jars and lids, sterilized

Combine raisins, flour, baking soda, baking powder, salt, cloves, cinnamon and ginger; set aside. In a large mixing bowl, blend together eggs, sugar, margarine and pumpkin; add dry ingredients. Pour into jars equally. Wipe rims clean; place on a baking sheet. Bake at 325 degrees for 40 minutes; remove from oven and immediately tighten down sterilized lids. Place jars on a wire rack to cool; check lids for seal. Makes 8 jars.

Paint a Jack-'O-Lantern face on a jar of Spicy Pumpkin Bread. Use black acrylic paint to add eyes, nose and a wide smile!

# Muffins & Breads

## Italian Zeppoli Bread

*This fried bread is an Italian Christmas Eve tradition.*

1 pkg. active dry yeast
1 c. warm water, divided
1-1/2 c. all-purpose flour

oil for deep frying
Garnish: powdered sugar

Dissolve yeast in 1/2 cup warm water; set aside for 10 minutes. Stir flour and remaining water into yeast mixture; beat until a soft dough forms. Turn dough onto a lightly floured surface; knead until smooth. Place in a greased bowl, turning once; cover with a damp cloth. Let rise in a warm place until double in bulk, about one to 1-1/2 hours. Fry 2-inch rounds of dough in 375-degree oil until golden. Drain on paper towels. Sprinkle with powdered sugar. Makes about 15.

Looking for a clever way to give a fresh-baked gift? Fill an old-fashioned sugar canister with Italian Zeppoli Bread...give with a shaker full of cinnamon and sugar.

# Cowboy Cornbread Mix

*A great addition to breakfast, lunch or dinner!*

| | |
|---|---|
| 1 c. all-purpose flour | 1 t. baking soda |
| 1 c. cornmeal | 1 T. baking powder |
| 1/4 c. sugar | 1/8 t. salt |

Combine ingredients together; store in an airtight container. Attach instructions. Makes 2-1/2 cups mix.

## Instructions:

Place cornbread mix in a large mixing bowl; set aside. Whisk 3 tablespoons melted and cooled butter and 1-1/3 cup buttermilk together in a separate bowl; add in one egg. Pour into cornbread mix; stir until just combined. Spread into a greased 8"x8" baking pan; bake at 425 degrees for 30 minutes. Makes 6 servings.

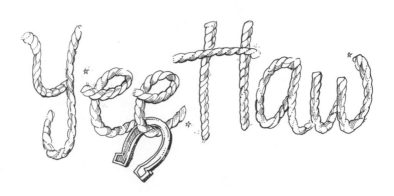

Pair a bag of Cowboy Cornbread Mix with a corn-on-the-cob cast iron pan and a chili recipe for a meal that's sure to be enjoyed.

# Muffins & Breads

## Western Surprise Bread

*Bread may also be baked in two, 8"x4" loaf pans at 325 degrees for 50 to 55 minutes.*

2 c. sugar
1 c. oil
3 eggs
16-oz. can pork & beans, drained
2 c. all-purpose flour
1-1/2 t. cinnamon
1/2 t. baking powder
1/2 t. baking soda
1 c. raisins
1 t. vanilla extract
5  16-oz. cans, rinsed, greased and floured

Mix sugar, oil, eggs and beans together until smooth; set aside. Combine flour, cinnamon, baking powder and baking soda in a mixing bowl; add to bean mixture. Fold in raisins; stir in vanilla. Fill cans 2/3 full with batter. Place cans on a baking sheet; bake at 325 degrees for 45 to 50 minutes. Cool completely before removing bread from cans. Makes 5 loaves.

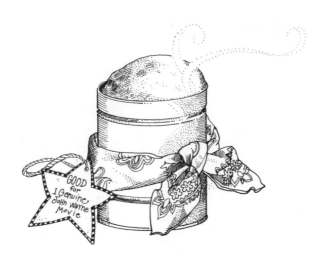

Great for Fathers' Day! Give a loaf of Western Surprise Bread along with a good old-fashioned cowboy movie.

# Savory Onion Bread

*Using a bread machine makes this loaf a cinch to prepare.*

3 c. whole-wheat flour
2-1/2 T. sugar
1-1/2 t. salt
2 T. wheat germ

2 t. active dry yeast
1-oz. pkg. dry onion soup mix
1 c. sour cream
1/2 c. water

Add ingredients to pan of bread machine in order suggested by the manufacturer; select dough cycle and press start. Remove dough from pan; shape dough. Place in a greased 9"x5" loaf pan; let rise to double in bulk in a warm place. Bake at 350 degrees for 30 minutes or until golden; cool. Makes 8 servings.

Deliver a loaf of Savory Onion Bread along with
some garlic butter to grandparents on
Grandparents' Day, September 9th.

# Muffins & Breads

## Garlic-Cheese Bread

*Perfect alongside any Italian dish.*

3-1/2 c. biscuit baking mix
2-3/4 c. shredded Cheddar
   cheese

1 t. garlic powder
1-1/4 c. milk
2 eggs, beaten

Combine all ingredients until just moistened; spread evenly into a greased 9"x5" loaf pan. Bake at 350 degrees for 30 to 40 minutes; cool on wire rack. Makes 8 servings.

## Cornmeal Tortillas

*It's so easy to make tortillas at home!*

1-1/2 c. cornmeal
1 c. all-purpose flour
1-1/4 t. salt

2 T. shortening
1/2 c. water

Combine cornmeal, flour and salt in a mixing bowl; cut in shortening to resemble course crumbs. Add water and stir with a fork until mixture becomes consistent and a ball is formed. Turn dough out onto a lightly floured, cloth-covered board; knead several times. Roll dough into 1-1/2 inch balls; let stand 15 minutes. Roll each ball into a 6-inch circle; place on ungreased baking sheets. Bake at 350 degrees for 15 minutes. Makes 12 tortillas.

# Nutty Date Bread

*Take this yummy bread to a friend's house with two mugs and some herbal tea...spend the afternoon catching up!*

1-1/2 c. hot water
1-1/2 c. pitted, chopped dates
2-3/4 c. all-purpose flour
2 t. baking soda
1 c. sugar

3/4 t. salt
1 T. butter, melted
1 egg, beaten
1 t. vanilla extract
1 c. chopped walnuts

Pour hot water over dates in a small bowl; set aside. Combine flour and baking soda together; add sugar and salt. Stir in cooled date mixture; stir well. Add butter, egg, vanilla and walnuts; mix well. Pour into a greased 9"x5" loaf pan; bake at 350 degrees for one hour or until bread tests done. Cool for 10 minutes before removing bread from loaf pan. Serves 8.

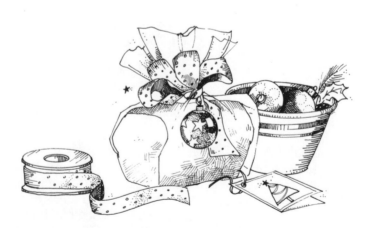

Bake several loaves of this sweet and nutty bread before the holidays. Freeze to have easy, last-minute gifts on hand.

# Muffins & Breads

## Bran-Raisin Muffin Mix

*Add an 8-ounce can of drained, crushed pineapple to the batter
for refreshing Pineapple-Bran Muffins.*

1-1/2 c. whole bran cereal
1-1/4 c. self-rising flour
1/2 c. sugar

1 c. golden raisins
1/4 t. salt

Mix ingredients together; store in an airtight container. Attach
instructions. Makes 4-1/4 cups mix.

## Instructions:

Combine muffin mix, 1/2 cup melted butter, 1/2 cup milk and one
beaten egg; mix until just moistened. Fill greased muffin cups 2/3 full.
Bake at 400 degrees for 16 to 18 minutes. Makes 12.

**Bran·Raisin Muffin Mix**

Combine muffin mix.
1/2 c. melted butter,
1/2 c. milk and
1 beaten egg.
Fill greased
muffin cups
2/3 full. Bake at 400° for 16-18 minutes. Makes 12.

Here's your instruction tag
to copy & tie on.

# Candied Fruit Loaf

*Colorful and sweet, this bread's a treat!*

2 eggs, beaten
1 c. milk
3 T. butter, melted
2 c. all-purpose flour
1 T. plus 1 t. baking powder
1/4 t. salt
1/4 t. cinnamon
3/4 c. sugar

1/4 c. candied citron, chopped
1/4 c. currants
2 T. candied cherries, chopped
2 T. candied lemon peel, chopped
1/4 c. chopped, blanched
   almonds
1/4 c. chopped pecans

Blend eggs, milk and butter together; set aside. Mix next 4 ingredients together; add sugar, fruits and nuts. Mix well. Combine egg mixture with fruit mixture; stir until just blended. Pour into a greased 8"x4" loaf pan; let stand for 20 minutes. Bake at 375 degrees for 60 to 70 minutes; cool on wire rack for several hours before slicing. Makes 8 servings.

For individual-size goodie gifts, slice a Candied Fruit Loaf,
stack three slices and wrap in wax paper or
tie with a wide ribbon.

# Muffins & Breads

## Apple Dapple Muffin Mix

*For a nuttier flavor, add 1/2 cup chopped walnuts
or pecans to the mix.*

2 c. self-rising flour
1/2 c. sugar
1/4 c. brown sugar, packed

2 t. cinnamon
1/4 t. nutmeg
1 c. dried apple, chopped

Combine ingredients together; store in an airtight container. Attach
instructions. Makes 4 cups.

### Instructions:

In a large mixing bowl, combine mix, one egg, 3/4 cup milk and
1/4 cup oil; stir until just moistened. Fill greased muffin tins 3/4 full.
Bake at 400 degrees until golden, about 15 to 18 minutes. Makes 12.

You're the apple of my eye!

Wrap a bag of
Apple Dapple
Muffin Mix in red
cellophane, tie it up
with green ribbon and
add a leaf-shaped gift tag.

# Homemade Graham Crackers

*Serve with a small bowl of homemade frosting for dipping!*

1/2 c. shortening
3/4 c. brown sugar, packed
1 t. vanilla extract
2 c. whole-wheat flour
1 c. all-purpose flour

1 t. baking powder
1/2 t. baking soda
1/8 t. salt
1/4 c. milk

In a medium mixing bowl, cream shortening and brown sugar together; stir in vanilla. In a separate bowl, combine flours, baking powder, baking soda and salt; stir into creamed mixture alternating with milk. Cover dough and chill until firm. On a lightly floured surface, roll dough to 1/8-inch thickness; cut into rectangles. Place each cracker 1/2 inch apart on greased baking sheets. Bake at 350 degrees for 10 to 12 minutes until edges are golden. Remove crackers from baking sheets to cool on wire racks. Makes 4 dozen.

S'mores on the go...pack Homemade Graham Crackers, chocolate candy bars and a jar of marshmallow creme. Yum!

Just copy,
cut·out & color!

In the end,
what affects your
**life** most
deeply
are the things too
**simple**
to talk about.

Neil Blane

Don't forget to
add the instructions
on the back.

to:

from:

from the Kitchen of:

Decoupage photos onto a tin for a one-of-a-kind package!

Set a snack Mix inside a clean paint can for a house warming present!

Welcome!

Snacks

Sample several snacks... Set paper baking cups in a Muffin tin & fill!

care packages...

Wrap up a spicy Mix in a bandanna and set down in a cowboy hat

Using poster board, create a Sampler by dividing a round tin into 6 sections.

Paint a plain glass candy dish to Match your occasion and fill!

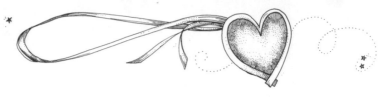

# Spicy Vanilla Pecans

*A wonderful snack for birthday and anniversary parties.*

1 lb. pecan halves
6 c. water
1/2 c. sugar
3 T. butter, melted
1 T. corn syrup
1 T. vanilla extract

1/4 t. salt
1/4 t. cinnamon
1/4 t. nutmeg
1/4 t. allspice
1/8 t. pepper

Boil pecans in water for one minute; drain. Immediately toss pecans in a large bowl with sugar, butter, corn syrup and vanilla; mix well. Cover bowl and let sit 12 to 24 hours. Place pecans on an ungreased jelly roll pan. Bake at 325 degrees for 30 minutes, stirring every 5 minutes. While pecans are baking, combine remaining ingredients in a large bowl. After baking pecans, immediately toss them with spices until well coated. Spread pecans on jelly roll pan in a single layer to allow for cooling. Makes one pound.

Old-fashioned glass jars are perfect containers for gifts from the kitchen. Jazz jars up by wrapping with layers of ribbon.

# Snacks

## Chewy Graham Popcorn

*Hostesses will love this sweet and crunchy treat...there's plenty to go around.*

10 c. popped popcorn
1-1/2 c. golden raisins
2-1/2 c. graham cracker cereal
1 c. mini marshmallows
1 c. chopped, dried dates

1/4 c. butter, melted
1/4 c. brown sugar, packed
2 t. cinnamon
1/2 t. ground ginger
1/2 t. nutmeg

Toss together first 5 ingredients; stir well. In a small bowl, combine remaining ingredients; stir into popcorn mixture. Pour mixture in a jelly roll pan; bake at 250 degrees for 20 minutes, stirring after 10 minutes. Cool. Makes about 3 quarts.

## Marshmallow Popcorn

*Chewy and sweet...this popcorn will be a welcome surprise in lunch boxes and briefcases!*

26 c. popped popcorn
1-1/4 c. salted peanuts
1/2 c. gumdrops

1/2 c. margarine
1/2 c. oil
9 c. mini marshmallows

In a large bowl, combine popcorn, peanuts and gumdrops; toss well. Over low heat, melt together margarine, oil and marshmallows, stir until melted. Pour over popcorn mixture to coat. Press into 2 greased jelly roll pans to cool. Makes about 2 gallons.

Present a tin filled with popcorn along with a board game or two...a gift for the entire family.

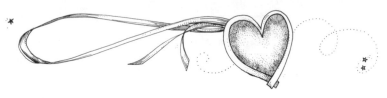

# Fruity Jelly Chews

*Mini cookie cutters are a quick & easy way to make fun animal-shaped chews.*

6 c. frozen raspberries
2 c. cranberries
1/3 c. water

3-1/2 c. sugar, divided
5 envelopes unflavored gelatin

Thaw raspberries in a bowl, saving juice. Press raspberries and juice through a fine strainer into another bowl; discard remaining pulp. In a 6 to 8-quart saucepan, combine raspberries, cranberries and water; bring to a boil over high heat, stirring constantly. Reduce heat and cover; simmer for 3 to 5 minutes, stirring occasionally, until cranberries are soft when pressed. Purée fruit mixture in a blender or food processor, a portion at a time until smooth; return to saucepan. In a separate bowl, combine 3 cups sugar and gelatin; add to fruit mixture. Bring mix to a boil over high heat, stirring often for 5 minutes. Reduce heat to medium and stir often until mixture is thick, about 15 to 20 minutes; remove from heat. Pour mixture into an oiled 8"x8" pan. Let candy dry, uncovered, for 16 to 24 hours until firm. On a sugar-coated surface, invert pan to release candy onto sugar. Cut candy into squares using a knife dipped in sugar. Place remaining sugar in a bowl; roll each square in sugar. Store in an airtight container with plastic wrap between layers. Makes 3 to 4 dozen pieces.

A mini fruit basket...line a small basket with a pretty towel and fill with fruity jelly chews. Wrap it all up in cellophane and tie with a bright bow.

# Snacks

## Classic Turtle Candy

*Pecans and caramel smothered in chocolate...yum!*

72 pecan halves
24 caramels, unwrapped
1-1/2 c. semi-sweet chocolate
   chips

1-1/2 t. shortening

Place 3 pecan halves in a Y-shape on greased baking sheets; place a caramel in the center. Repeat with remaining nuts and caramels. Bake at 300 degrees for 10 minutes until caramels are melted. In a small saucepan, melt chocolate chips and shortening over low heat, stirring until smooth. Spoon chocolate over candies on baking sheets. Chill overnight, until firm. Makes 2 dozen.

Look for a small fish bowl at a pet store...it's a clever package for Classic Turtle Candy!

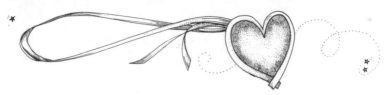

## Fruit Basket Salsa

*Pair with Cinnamon Crunchies for a good-for-you gift!*

1 pt. strawberries, hulled
   and sliced
1 banana, sliced
1 apple, cored, peeled and diced
1 kiwi, peeled and sliced

1/4 c. lemon juice
1 T. lime juice
1/4 c. sugar
1/4 t. nutmeg
1/2 t. cinnamon

Combine fruit in a large mixing bowl. In a separate bowl, stir together remaining ingredients; pour over fruit, tossing well. Chill. Serves 4.

## Cinnamon Crunchies

*Light and crispy!*

4 flour tortillas
3/4 t. cinnamon

2 T. sugar

Cut each tortilla into 8 wedges; place on ungreased baking sheets. Combine cinnamon and sugar; sprinkle over tortillas. Bake at 350 degrees for 6 to 8 minutes or until golden. Makes 32 chips.

For a clever hostess gift, place Fruit Basket Salsa and Cinnamon Crunchies in a decorative chip & dip bowl.

# Snacks

## Sugar & Spice Pumpkin Seeds

*Great Halloween treat...easy to make after carving pumpkins.*

5 T. sugar, divided
1/4 t. coarse salt
1/4 t. cumin
1/2 t. cinnamon

1/4 t. ground ginger
1/8 t. cayenne pepper
1-1/2 T. peanut oil
1 c. pumpkin seeds, baked

In a medium bowl, combine 3 tablespoons sugar, salt, cumin, cinnamon, ginger and cayenne. Heat peanut oil in a large skillet over high heat; add pumpkin seeds and remaining sugar. Cook until sugar melts and pumpkin seeds begin to caramelize, about one minute. Pour seeds in bowl with spices, stirring well to coat; let cool. Store in an airtight container. Makes one cup.

Fill small paper bags with Sugar & Spice Pumpkin Seeds for a tasty trick-or-treat bag or set out a plastic pumpkin filled with these treats for guests to enjoy.

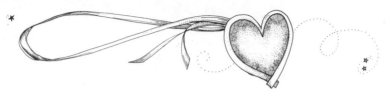

# Buncha Crunch Snack Mix

*Kids love this nutritious combination of cereal and pretzels!*

2 c. bite-size crispy wheat cereal
squares
2 c. bite-size crispy rice cereal
squares
2 c. bite-size cheese crackers
2 c. pretzel squares

1 c. doughnut-shaped oat cereal
1 c. peanuts
5 T. Worcestershire sauce
2 t. seasoned salt
1 t. garlic powder
1 t. onion powder

Combine first 6 ingredients in a large roasting pan and spray with olive oil cooking spray; toss to coat. Add Worcestershire sauce one tablespoon at a time, stirring after each addition. Stir in seasoned salt, garlic and onion powder. Bake at 250 degrees for one hour, stirring every 15 minutes. Cool mixture on paper towels. Store in an airtight container. Makes 10 cups.

# Spicy Tex-Mex Mix

*A snacky treat with a Mexican twist.*

2-1/2 c. lightly salted peanuts
3 c. corn chips
3 c. shredded wheat cereal
2-1/2 c. lightly salted pretzels

1-1/4 oz. pkg. taco seasoning
mix
1/4 c. butter, melted

Combine all ingredients in a large bowl; toss well to coat. Store in an airtight container. Makes 11 cups.

A thoughtful shower gift! Fill a set of clear, stemmed glasses with different types of snacks. Cover each with plastic wrap and tie a bow around the stem to secure.

# Snacks

## Tortilla Roll-Ups

*These savory snacks make any day feel like a special occasion.*

8-oz. pkg. cream cheese
1 c. sour cream
1/4 c. honey
1 T. canned chili peppers
1/4 c. green peppers, chopped

1/4 c. onion, chopped
1/2 t. onion powder
1/2 t. garlic powder
1/2 c. shredded Cheddar cheese
10 flour tortillas

Beat together cream cheese, sour cream and honey until smooth; stir in remaining ingredients. Spread equal amounts of mixture onto each tortilla. Roll up each tortilla; place in a covered dish and chill for 2 hours. Slice each roll into one-inch pieces; place on a platter. Refrigerate until serving. Makes 4 dozen pinwheels.

A great gift for Dad! Give a platter of Tortilla Roll-Ups with a coupon good for an indoor tailgating party...uninterrupted football coverage complete with his favorite snacks and drinks.

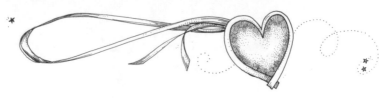

# Italian Bagel Chips

*A flavorful crunch from a baked chip.*

9 frozen mini bagels, thawed
1-1/2 t. Italian seasoning
1/4 t. onion powder

1/4 t. garlic powder
salt and pepper to taste

Cut each bagel crosswise into 4 slices. Place slices in a single layer on an ungreased baking sheet; lightly coat tops with non-stick cooking vegetable spray. In a small bowl, combine remaining ingredients; sprinkle evenly over bagels. Bake at 375 degrees for 12 minutes or until crisp. Makes 3 dozen chips.

Blend together a packet of ranch dressing mix
and cream cheese...give with Italian Bagel Chips
for a delightful surprise.

# Snacks

## Savory Garlic Almonds

*So quick, so easy...so tasty!*

1 T. butter
2 T. soy sauce
2 t. hot pepper sauce
3 cloves garlic, pressed

1 lb. blanched whole almonds
3 t. pepper
1 T. seasoned salt
1/4 t. red pepper flakes

Coat a jelly roll pan with butter; set aside. Sprinkle soy sauce, hot pepper sauce and garlic in a mixing bowl; add almonds, stirring until well coated. Pour mixture in a single layer into jelly roll pan. Bake at 350 degrees for 10 minutes. Sprinkle almonds with remaining ingredients. Bake for 15 minutes; cool in pan. Store in an airtight container. Makes about one pound.

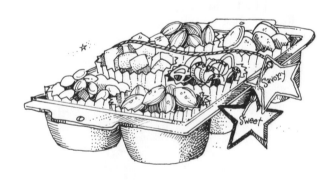

A quick & easy sampler of snacks! Place several paper muffin liners, side by side, in a large muffin tin...fill each with a different treat. Try a sampler including a sweet mix with candy, these Savory Garlic Almonds and a hearty trail mix...yum!

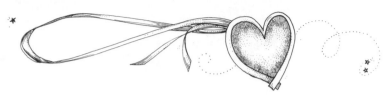

# Caramel Popcorn in a Jar

*A quick and inexpensive gift!*

1 c. sugar
1 c. brown sugar, packed
1-1/3 c. unpopped popcorn

14-oz. can sweetened condensed milk

Layer sugar and brown sugar in a one-quart, wide-mouth jar, packing down as tightly as possible. Place popcorn into a small plastic zipping bag; seal bag and place on top of sugar. Secure jar lid. Using clear packing tape, firmly attach the can of milk to the bottom of the jar. Tie on instructions.

## Instructions:

Remove popcorn from jar and pop in a covered, 4-quart saucepan using 2 tablespoons oil. Shake constantly until popping stops; discard unpopped kernels. In a separate saucepan, mix together sugars, milk and 1/2 cup butter; bring to a boil, stirring constantly. Boil for one minute; remove from heat. Immediately pour mixture over popcorn; toss until all corn is well coated. Spread onto greased baking sheets to cool. Makes about 20 cups.

Send Caramel Popcorn in a Jar along with kids heading off to slumber parties...the kids will have a fun treat and the host will appreciate the easy snack!

# Snacks

## Chocolate-Peanut Popcorn

*Milk chocolate and popcorn...all you need is a good movie!*

12 c. popped popcorn
2-1/4 c. salted peanuts
1-3/4 c. milk chocolate chips

1 c. corn syrup
1/4 c. butter

Combine popcorn and nuts in a greased roasting pan; set aside. In a heavy saucepan, melt together chocolate chips, corn syrup and butter, stirring constantly. Bring mixture to a boil; pour over popcorn, tossing well to coat. Bake at 300 degrees for 30 to 40 minutes, stirring every 10 minutes. Remove from oven, stir and allow to cool slightly in pan. Remove popcorn to a baking sheet lined with wax paper to cool completely. Store in an airtight container. Makes 14 cups.

Create a gift bag with a window. Cut a shape from the front of the bag and glue cellophane or plastic wrap on the inside to cover the opening...a sneak peek at the treats.

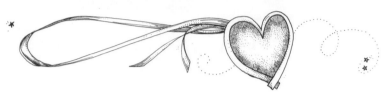

# Melt-in-Your-Mouth Candy

*This toffee is an easy treat that's sure to please.*

1-1/4 c. sugar
1 c. corn syrup
1 T. vinegar

1 T. baking soda
1 lb. melting chocolate

Combine sugar, corn syrup and vinegar in a medium saucepan over medium heat, stirring until sugar dissolves. Heat without stirring to the hard-crack stage, or 290 to 310 degrees on a candy thermometer; remove from heat. Stir in baking soda. Pour mixture into a greased 13"x9" pan; do not spread. Allow to cool completely. Melt chocolate in a double boiler, stirring until smooth. Break cooled candy into bite-size pieces and spread out on wax paper. Drizzle melted chocolate over candy until completely coated. Store in an airtight container. Makes 1-1/2 pounds.

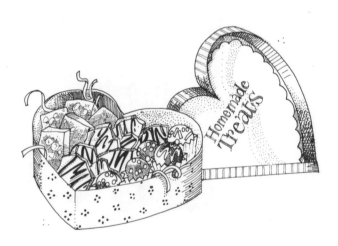

Fill a candy box with homemade treats and make a special menu of what's inside...just like the store-bought candy samplers!

## Heavenly Truffles

*These colorful sweets are perfect for a child's birthday party.*

1 c. creamy peanut butter
1/2 c. corn syrup
1 c. crispy rice cereal

8-oz. chocolate bar, broken into
   pieces
1/4 c. colorful sprinkles

Beat together peanut butter and corn syrup in a large bowl; stir in cereal until well mixed. Line a baking sheet with wax paper. Shape teaspoonfuls of peanut butter mixture into balls; place on wax paper. Refrigerate 2 hours until firm. Melt chocolate in a double boiler, stirring constantly until smooth. Using a fork, dip each peanut butter ball in chocolate then roll in colored sprinkles. Return truffles to wax paper; refrigerate one hour until firm. Makes 3-1/2 dozen.

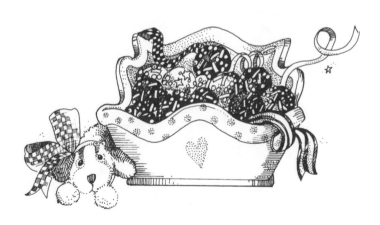

Give a cozy night by the fireplace! Fill an ice bucket with sparkling juice, drinking glasses and these Heavenly Truffles.

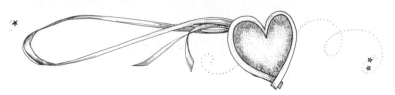

## Oh-So-Rich Buckeyes

*No one will guess the secret ingredient...graham crackers!*

2 c. creamy peanut butter
1 c. graham cracker crumbs
2 c. powdered sugar

4 c. semi-sweet chocolate chips
4 T. shortening

Combine peanut butter, graham cracker crumbs and powdered sugar, mixing until smooth; refrigerate at least one hour. Roll teaspoonfuls of peanut butter mixture into balls and place on wax paper; refrigerate until ready to dip. Melt chocolate chips and shortening in a double boiler, stirring until smooth. Insert a toothpick in the peanut butter balls and dip in chocolate until 3/4 covered. Return to wax paper to cool. Makes 5 dozen.

Surprise friends with some homemade Oh-So-Rich Buckeyes on their anniversary. Package in a vintage tin or decoupage a wedding picture onto the lid of a plain or painted tin found at craft stores. Use ribbon to tie on a gift tag that reads, "To a sweet couple...May your years together be oh-so rich!"

## Chocolate-Covered Peanuts

*Last-minute dinner invitation? Whip up these yummy clusters and tuck in a vintage tin for the hosts.*

1 c. semi-sweet chocolate chips
1/4 c. corn syrup

1 T. water
2 c. salted peanuts

Combine chocolate, corn syrup and water in a double boiler; stir until melted. Remove from heat and stir in peanuts until well coated. Drop mixture by teaspoonfuls onto baking sheets lined with wax paper. Cover baking sheets with aluminum foil and chill until firm. Makes 3 dozen.

Dainty pouches can be sewn from broad bands of ribbon. Arrange ribbon in a basket weave pattern, stitch at the sides, leaving the top open for filling. Trim the excess and tie on a handle of silky ribbon. Slip almonds or chocolate-covered peanuts into a plastic zipping bag and tuck inside the ribbon pouch...so pretty for bridal showers or weddings.

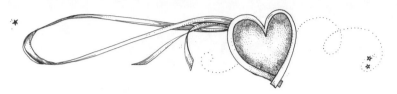

# Dreamy Peanut Brittle

*An old-fashioned favorite.*

3 c. sugar
1 c. corn syrup
1/2 c. water
4-1/2 c. salted peanuts

4 T. butter
1/2 T. vanilla extract
2 t. baking soda

In a heavy 5-quart saucepan, combine sugar, corn syrup and water; cover and bring to a boil over high heat, about 5 minutes. Swirl the pot often over the burner to dissolve the sugar. Once steam begins to rise around the lid, remove it and reduce heat to medium. Continue to boil for one minute to the thread stage, or 230 to 233 degrees on a candy thermometer. Add peanuts; stir constantly with a metal spoon until mixture reaches the hard-crack stage, or 290 to 310 degrees on a candy thermometer, about 13 to 18 minutes. Immediately remove pan from heat and quickly add butter, vanilla and baking soda; stir until mixture becomes foamy. Pour into two, 17"x12" baking pans coated with a non-stick vegetable spray. Evenly spread mixture with a spatula; allow to cool for at least one hour. Turn brittle out of pan; snap it into bite-size pieces. Store in an airtight container. Makes 2 pounds.

Buy an inexpensive plastic truck or wagon at a toy store...fill the bed with peanut brittle and tie on a tag that says, "To a friend who's loads of fun."

# Snacks

## One-of-a-Kind Toffee

*One taste of this scrumptious candy and you'll understand the name.*

1 lb. butter
1 c. sugar
1 c. brown sugar, packed

1 c. chopped pecans
2 c. semi-sweet chocolate chips

In a heavy saucepan, combine butter and sugars. Cook over medium heat, stirring constantly until mixture boils. Without stirring, boil to hard-crack stage, or 290 to 310 degrees on a candy thermometer; remove from heat. Pour walnuts and chocolate chips into a lightly greased 13"x9" pan; pour hot butter mixture on top. Allow mixture to cool completely; break into pieces before serving. Makes 8 servings.

Vellum bags turn simple treats into charming gifts...look
for them at a craft or stationery store. Fill with
One-of-a-Kind Toffee, fold the top
over to close and seal with a sticker.

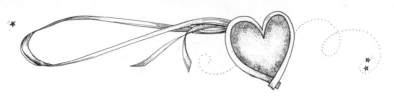

# Chocolate-Dipped Cherries

*These are tastiest after sitting for a week...if you can stand the wait!*

2-1/2 c. powdered sugar
1/4 c. butter, softened
1 T. milk
1/4 t. almond extract

2  8-oz. jars maraschino cherries
    with stems, drained
2 c. semi-sweet chocolate chips
2 T. shortening

Mix together sugar, butter, milk and almond extract; knead into a large ball. Roll into one-inch balls and flatten each into a 2-inch circle. Wrap each circle around a cherry and lightly roll in hands. Place balls, stem up, on a baking sheet lined with wax paper; cover loosely and refrigerate overnight. Melt chocolate chips and shortening in a double boiler. Holding onto each stem, dip cherries into chocolate; return to wax paper to harden. Refrigerate in an airtight container for one to 2 weeks before serving to allow for a juicy center.
Makes 3 dozen.

Send flowers and Chocolate-Dipped Cherries to
a sweetie the day before an anniversary or
Valentine's Day...enclose a note saying,
"I just couldn't wait 'til tomorrow."

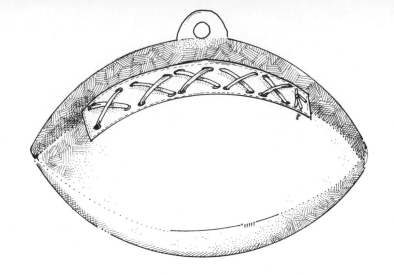

(Write your instructions in the middle of the bandanna.)

Don't forget to write the ☆ instructions ✱ on the back!

A little of what you fancy does you G·O·O·D.

Marie — Lloyd —

Copy, color & tie on!

OH·SO ~GOOD~ from:

from the kitchen of:

Tuck a coffee mix down inside a thermos

Warm 'em up with cocoa mix inside a new pair of mittens.

COCOA

Cocoa, Coffee & Tea

Give fire starters with your cocoa!

Tie spoons together with ribbon and place inside an oversized mug.

Tuck teabags into a teacup and add a stack of mug mats....cozy

for you!

# Easy Toffee-Coffee Mix

*A sweet and creamy treat!*

2/3 c. instant coffee granules
1 c. powdered non-dairy creamer
1 c. brown sugar, packed
1 T. toffee pieces, crushed

Combine all ingredients in a large bowl; store in an airtight container. Attach instructions. Makes 3 cups mix.

## Instructions:

Use 2 to 3 teaspoons of mix for every one cup boiling water. Makes one serving.

# Chocolate Stirring Spoons

*An easy gift to make for the coffee lovers on your list.*

12-oz. pkg. semi-sweet
   chocolate chips
2 t. shortening
35 to 45 plastic spoons

Line baking sheets with parchment paper. Place chocolate chips in a microwave-safe bowl; microwave on medium power for 2 minutes or until melted, stirring every thirty seconds. To thin chocolate, add shortening to chocolate; gently stir. Dip each plastic spoon in chocolate mixture to cover the bowl of the spoon; place on parchment paper to set. Cool thoroughly before wrapping. Makes 35 to 45 spoons.

# Cocoa, Coffee & Tea

## Minty Hot Cocoa Mix

*Three times the chocolate!*

1-1/4 c. powdered milk
1/4 c. hot chocolate mix
1/4 c. mint chocolate chips

2 T. powdered chocolate
   non-dairy creamer
1 t. cinnamon

Mix all ingredients; pour into a one-pint jar. Attach a gift tag with instructions. Makes 2 cups mix.

## Instructions:

Place 1/3 cup mixture into a mug; add one cup boiling water. Stir until mint chips are melted. Makes one serving.

Fill an old-fashioned milk bottle with Minty Hot Cocoa Mix...look for them at flea markets and antique shops.

# Spicy Fruit Tea Mix

*This flavorful treat is great hot or cold.*

15-oz. container orange
    drink mix
1 c. sugar
1 c. unsweetened instant tea mix
1/2 c. sweetened lemonade
    drink mix

1/4-oz. pkg. unsweetened
    raspberry-flavored drink mix
2 t. cinnamon
1 t. nutmeg

Combine all ingredients; mix well. Store in an airtight container. Attach instructions. Makes 5-1/2 cups mix.

## Instructions:

Stir 2 tablespoons mix into one cup of hot or cold water. Makes one serving.

Place a bag of Spicy
Fruit Tea Mix in
a pretty mug or
teapot...tie on a few
colorful stir sticks and
attach a gift tag.

## Cranberry Cider Mix

*So cozy!*

1/2 c. sweetened, dried
    cranberries
12 cinnamon sticks

1/2 t. ground cloves
1 T. whole allspice
1 T. nutmeg

Mix together all ingredients. Store in an airtight container. Attach instructions for giving. Makes about 1-1/2 cups mix.

## Instructions:

In a large saucepan, combine 2 quarts apple cider, one quart water and cranberry cider mix; heat until warm. Add 2 sliced oranges. Makes 3 quarts.

Fill an old-fashioned crock with Cranberry Cider Mix and take it to a party...it'll make more than enough!

# Orange-Spice Cappuccino Mix

*A refreshing change from ordinary cappuccino.*

1/2 c. powdered non-dairy
   creamer
1/2 c. sugar

1/4 c. instant coffee granules
2 t. dried orange zest
1 t. cinnamon

Combine all ingredients in a blender or food processor; blend until well mixed. Store in an airtight container and attach instructions. Makes about 2-1/4 cups mix.

## Instructions:

Place 2 teaspoons mix and 2/3 cup boiling water in a mug, stirring well. Makes one serving.

An afternoon for two! Take Orange-Spice Cappuccino Mix,
2 mugs and a good movie over to a friend's house...a great
way to spend the day.

## Rich & Creamy Mocha Mix

*Enjoy a cup of with friends over a board game.*

1-1/2 c. powdered milk
1/2 c. instant coffee granules
1 t. vanilla powder

1/3 c. brown sugar, packed
3/4 c. mini milk chocolate chips

Combine ingredients, mixing to combine. Store in an airtight container. Tie on a gift tag with instructions. Makes 3 cups mix.

### Instructions:

In a blender, combine 1/4 cup mix with 2/3 cup boiling water. Blend until frothy; pour in a mug. Makes one serving.

Morning surprise! Leave a mug filled with Rich & Creamy Mocha Mix on a co-worker's desk for her to enjoy when she arrives.

# Pepperminty Coffee Mix

*This minty mix makes a delightful after-dinner coffee.*

1/3 c. sugar
1/4 c. powdered non-dairy
   creamer

1/4 c. instant coffee granules
2 T. baking cocoa
2 T. peppermint candy, crushed

Combine all ingredients; store in an airtight container. Attach instructions before giving. Makes about one cup mix.

## Instructions:

Combine 2 tablespoons mix with 1/2 cup boiling water; mix well. Makes one serving.

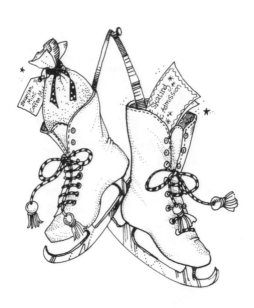

Pair Pepperminty Coffee Mix with ice skating passes
for a clever stocking stuffer.

# Cocoa, Coffee & Tea

## Marshmallow Cocoa Mix

*This quick & easy cocoa is a favorite of kids of all ages.*

25-oz. pkg. powdered milk
1-1/2 c. powdered non-dairy
　creamer
3 c. hot cocoa mix

1-1/2 c. powdered sugar
2 c. mini marshmallows

Combine ingredients; equally divide into four, one-quart jars. Attach gift tags with instructions to each. Makes 4 jars.

### Instructions:

Combine 1/2 cup mix with one cup boiling water. Makes one serving.

## Candy Cane Stirrers

*These handy stirrers will hang right on the edge of a cocoa mug!*

6-oz. pkg. semi-sweet chocolate
　chips, divided

50 mini peppermint candy canes

In a small microwave-safe bowl, heat 3/4 cup chocolate chips in a microwave on low power for 1-1/2 minutes. Stir chocolate until smooth; heat for 20 more seconds if necessary. Add remaining chocolate and stir until smooth. Set bowl in a pan of hot water to keep chocolate soft, making sure water does not mix with chocolate. Dip straight end of each candy cane into chocolate to coat; lay on wax paper to cool. Wrap each candy cane in clear plastic wrap. Makes 50.

# Southern Peach Tea Mix

*Pair with a rich, buttery pound cake...so yummy!*

1 c. instant tea mix
3-oz. box instant peach-flavored
   gelatin

2 c. sugar

Combine all ingredients, mixing well. Store in an airtight container.
Attach instructions before giving. Makes 3-1/2 cups.

## Instructions:

Combine 2 teaspoons tea mix with one cup hot water in a mug. Makes
one serving.

# Friendship Sip Mix

*Try this fruity drink over ice for a warm-weather beverage.*

2 c. orange drink mix
1 c. lemonade drink mix
1-1/3 c. sugar

1-1/2 t. cinnamon
1/2 t. ground cloves

Mix all ingredients together; store in an airtight container. Tie on a gift
tag with instructions. Makes about 4 cups mix.

## Instructions:

Mix 2 tablespoons mix into one cup boiling water; stir. Makes
one serving.

## Homemade Lemonade Mix

*This summertime favorite is perfect year 'round.*

3 c. sugar
1 c. boiling water

3 c. lemon juice
2 T. lemon zest

Combine sugar and water in a stockpot, stirring until sugar dissolves; cool. Add lemon juice and zest; mix well. Cover and refrigerate; use mix within one week. Attach instructions. Makes about 6 cups mix.

## Instructions:

Combine 1/3 cup lemonade mix with 3/4 cup cold water; stir well. Makes one serving.

← Copy & attach!

Homemade
Lemonade Mix

Combine 1/3 cup lemonade mix
with 3/4 cup cold water;
stir well.
Makes 1 serving.

Create a dinner kit for a new mom! Bring over a
warm casserole, paper plates and cups, plastic
utensils and Homemade Lemonade Mix.

# Hot Chocolate Malt Mix

*A hot chocolate lover's dream!*

25-oz. pkg. powdered milk
16-oz. jar powdered non-dairy
   creamer
16-oz. jar hot chocolate mix

13-oz. jar malted milk powder
1 c. powdered sugar
1 t. vanilla powder
2 c. mini marshmallows

Use a wire whisk to combine all ingredients. Equally divide mix into 4 plastic zipping bags and attach instructions to each. Makes about 13 cups.

## Instructions:

Place 3 tablespoons mix into a mug. Add one cup boiling water; stir well. Makes one serving.

Here's your instruction tag to copy & tie on.

"No act of kindness, no matter how small, is ever wasted." Aesop

# Thanks!

To:                          from:

COLD HANDS WARM HEARTS!

MARS

One sip of this will bathe drooping spirits in delight beyond the bliss of dreams. ~MILTON~

to:                          from:

to:

from:

The most wasted of
all days is that
in which we have not

laughed.

- Chamfort -

to:

from your friend:

Fill a new colander with dry pasta & Italian Seasonings

Italian Seasoning

Slip marinade mixes or barbeque seasonings inside an oven mitt.

Dips & Seasonings

always the perfect gift for a party!

congrats

DIP

Add a stack of ramekins tied with a bow to create a great gift.

Set herb dips or blends inside terra cotta pots & place in a vintage carrier.

taco

←ruffled

# Creamy Lemon Fruit Dip

*Surprise your hostess with a fruit tray and this dip.*

2 eggs
1 c. sugar, divided
1/3 c. lemon juice
1 T. cornstarch

1/2 c. water
1-1/2 t. vanilla extract
1 c. whipping cream, whipped

In a mixing bowl, beat together eggs, 1/2 cup sugar and lemon juice. In a saucepan, combine remaining sugar and cornstarch; stir in water. Cook and stir until thickened; remove from heat. Gradually beat in egg mixture. Over low heat, cook and stir until slightly thickened. Add vanilla; cool. Fold in whipped cream. Makes about 4 cups.

New neighbor on the block? Surprise them with a
basket of fresh fruit along with a crock full of
this Creamy Lemon Fruit Dip...they'll love it!

# Dips & Seasonings

## Honey-Cinnamon Fluff

*This fruit dip is rich, creamy and irresistible.*

8-oz. pkg. cream cheese,
    softened
7-oz. jar marshmallow creme

1 T. honey
1/2 t. cinnamon

In a small bowl, combine all ingredients; beat until smooth. Store in an airtight container in the refrigerator. Makes 1-1/2 cups.

## Piña Colada Fruit Dip

*Be sure you attach the recipe when giving this dip...it's a hit!*

1/2 c. plain yogurt
1/3 c. crushed pineapple,
    drained

2 T. flaked coconut
1 t. sugar

Combine all ingredients in a small bowl; stir until smooth. Store in an airtight container and chill before serving. Makes about one cup.

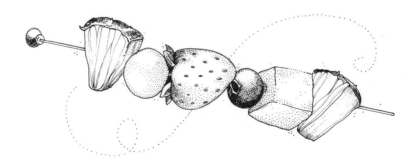

# True Blueberry Joy

*Spread on French toast and warm muffins.*

1-1/2 t. unflavored gelatin
3/4 c. water, divided
2 c. blueberries
2 t. lemon juice

3-1/2 T. sugar
2  1/2-pint canning jars and
    lids, sterilized

Sprinkle gelatin over 1/4 cup cold water; set aside. Combine
blueberries, remaining water and lemon juice in a heavy saucepan;
bring to a boil over medium-high heat. Reduce heat; simmer for
8 minutes, stirring often. Stir in gelatin mixture and sugar until
dissolved. Pour into jars; wipe rims and seal with lids. Cool and store
in refrigerator. Makes 2 jars.

# Pumpkin Butter

*What a welcome harvest gift!*

29-oz. can pumpkin
2/3 c. apple juice
2 t. ground ginger
1/2 t. ground cloves
1-1/2 c. sugar

2 t. cinnamon
1/2 t. nutmeg
5  1/2-pint canning jars and
    lids, sterilized

Combine all ingredients in a heavy saucepan; bring to a boil. Reduce
heat; simmer until thickened, about 30 to 40 minutes, stirring
frequently. Spoon into jars filling to within 1/4 inch from the top; run a
knife through the mixture to remove air bubbles. Wipe jar rims; cover
with lids. Process in a boiling water bath for 10 minutes. Makes 5 jars.

# Dips & Seasonings

## Old-Fashioned Gooseberry Jelly

*Tart, sweet and just right.*

8 c. gooseberries, mashed
6 c. sugar
1 T. lemon zest

6-oz. bottle liquid pectin
10  1/2-pint canning jars
    and lids, sterilized

Place gooseberries in a heavy saucepan. Stir in sugar and zest; bring to a full boil over high heat, stirring constantly. Boil for one minute; remove from heat. Mix in pectin; skim off any foam with a metal spoon. Stir and skim mixture frequently for 5 minutes; spoon into hot jars to within 1/4 inch from the jar top. Wipe rims and seal with lid. Process in a hot water bath for 10 minutes. Makes 10 jars.

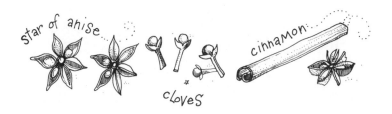

## Kiwi-Citrus Jam

*Perfect for morning toast or spread on bagels.*

24 kiwis, peeled and mashed
2/3 c. pineapple juice
1/4 c. lemon juice
3 apples, cored and halved

4 c. sugar
5  1/2-pint canning jars
    and lids, sterilized

Measure 3 cups mashed kiwis; add to a heavy saucepan with juice and apples. Bring mixture to a boil; add sugar, stirring until dissolved. Reduce heat; simmer for 30 minutes. Remove apples and discard; pour mixture into jars. Wipe rims and seal with lids. Process in a hot water bath for 10 minutes. Makes 5 jars.

## Hot Fudge Sauce

*Not just for sundaes...try it over creamy cheesecake too.*

3/4 c. whipping cream
1/4 c. butter, sliced
1/4 c. sugar
1/4 c. brown sugar, packed
1/8 t. salt

1/2 c. baking cocoa
1-1/2 t. vanilla extract
1-oz. sq. semi-sweet baking
   chocolate, chopped

Combine cream and butter in a heavy saucepan; heat over medium heat until boiling. Stir in sugars until dissolved; remove from heat, blend in remaining ingredients. Heat until warmed, whisking until smooth. Makes 1-1/2 cups.

## Hot Mocha Fudge

*Just a hint of coffee sets this sauce apart.*

4  1-oz. sqs. unsweetened
   baking chocolate, melted
1 c. sugar

1/2 c. evaporated milk
1 T. coffee
1 t. vanilla extract

Combine chocolate and sugar in a double boiler; cover and bring to a gentle boil for 1/2 hour. Remove from heat; whisk in remaining ingredients until thick and smooth. Makes 2 cups.

# Dips & Seasonings

## Peanut Butter Sauce

*Serve warm over ice cream!*

1 c. butter, melted
2 c. brown sugar, packed

5-oz. can evaporated milk
1-1/4 c. creamy peanut butter

Combine all ingredients in a saucepan; heat over medium heat until sugar dissolves. Heat and stir until smooth and creamy. Makes about 5 cups.

## Cinnamon-Spice Sprinkle

*Sprinkle on sliced fruit, pudding and in muffin cups before adding batter.*

10 T. sugar, divided
1 t. cinnamon
1 t. ground ginger

1 t. ground cardamom
1 t. ground coriander
1 t. nutmeg

Layer spices into a one-cup narrow, clear jar. Makes about 3/4 cup. Attach instructions.

### Instructions:

Shake gently until well blended.

# Backyard-Barbecue Mango Chutney

*So tasty on chicken, pork chops and even fish!*

3 c. white vinegar
6 c. sugar
6 c. brown sugar, packed
2 t. cinnamon
2 t. ground ginger
1-1/2 T. allspice
1-1/2 t. ground cloves
2 t. nutmeg
4 red hot chili peppers, seeded
   and chopped

1 t. kosher salt
2 onions, chopped
3 cloves garlic, chopped
1 c. golden raisins
1 c. raisins
16 c. mangos, peeled and sliced
1/2 c. sliced almonds
4　1-quart canning jars and
   lids, sterilized

Combine first 10 ingredients in a large saucepan; boil for 30 minutes.
Add onions, garlic, golden raisins and raisins; boil for another
30 minutes. Reduce heat; stir in mangos and almonds. Simmer
mixture for 30 minutes; pour into jars to within 1/2 inch from rims.
Wipe rims; add lids and seal. Process in a hot water bath for
10 minutes. Makes 4 jars.

A jar of fresh Backyard-Barbecue Mango Chutney makes a
nice gift for grillers...add tongs, an oven mitt and grill brush.

# Dips & Seasonings

## Spicy Pepper Jelly

*Serve with cream cheese and crackers for a tasty spread.*

3/4 c. green pepper, finely
   chopped
3/4 c. red pepper, finely chopped
1-1/2 c. white vinegar
6-1/2 c. sugar

6 T. liquid pectin
2 1-pint canning jars and
  lids, sterilized

Combine peppers, vinegar and sugar in a stainless steel saucepan; boil for 6 minutes, stirring constantly. Add pectin; continue to boil for 3 additional minutes, stirring constantly. Remove from heat; skim foam using a metal spoon. Ladle into hot, sterilized jars to within 1/2 inch from the top; wipe rims, add lids and seal. Process in a boiling water bath for 5 minutes; set jars aside to cool. Makes 2 jars.

Surprise a favorite gardener with the freshest picks from the pepper patch along with a jar of Spicy Pepper Jelly!

## Cajun Spice Mix

*Sprinkle this mix on eggs, potatoes and meat dishes...yum!*

2/3 c. salt, divided
1/4 c. cayenne pepper, divided
2 T. white pepper
2 T. pepper

2 T. paprika
2 T. onion powder
2 T. garlic powder

Layer in a pint jar in desired order, dividing salt and cayenne pepper into several layers. Makes 1-1/2 cups.

## Brown Sugar Barbecue Rub

*Generously coat chicken, fish fillets or ribs before grilling.*

1/4 c. brown sugar, packed
1/4 c. coriander seed, toasted
   and crushed
1/4 c. paprika

1/4 c. cumin
1 t. garlic salt
1/8 t. pepper

Combine ingredients together in a small bowl; mix well. Makes about one cup.

# Dips & Seasonings

## Go-Team Chili Seasoning

*Give this seasoning mix with a stack of soup bowls or a new stockpot...just right for housewarmings.*

| | |
|---|---|
| 1 T. all-purpose flour | 1/2 t. cayenne pepper |
| 2 T. dried, minced onion | 1/2 t. garlic powder |
| 1-1/2 t. chili powder | 1 t. sugar |
| 1 t. salt | 1/2 t. cumin |

Mix all ingredients together; store in an airtight container. Attach instructions. Makes 1/4 cup.

## Instructions:

Brown one pound ground beef in a skillet; drain. Add seasoning mix, two, 15-1/2 ounce cans kidney beans and two, 16-ounce cans stewed tomatoes. Reduce heat; simmer for 10 minutes, stirring occasionally. Makes 4 to 6 servings.

Chili makes a hearty tailgating meal so why not give this seasoning mix a few days before a big game? Decorate the container with pennants of the opposing teams.

## Sweet, Hot & Tangy Sauce

*Great as a dipping sauce for grilled chicken, ham and shrimp.*

5-oz. jar horseradish sauce
1.12-oz. can dry mustard
18-oz. jar pineapple preserves

18-oz. jar apple jelly
1 T. coarse pepper
1/2 t. poppy seed

Mix horseradish sauce and dry mustard together; add remaining ingredients until well blended. Store covered; keep refrigerated. Makes about 5 cups.

## Hot Jalapeño Jam

*Mix with sour cream for a yummy dip.*

12 jalapeño peppers, seeded
    and halved
2 tomatoes
boiling water
1 onion, finely chopped

1 green apple, cored and grated
1/2 c. red wine vinegar
2/3 c. sugar
1/2 t. pepper

Arrange pepper halves on a broiler pan; broil until skins are blackened. Remove; cover with a towel and set aside until cool. Slice an "X" in the base of both tomatoes; place in a small bowl and cover with boiling water for 2 minutes. Drain and cool. Peel and discard skins from peppers and tomatoes; finely chop peppers and tomatoes. Combine with remaining ingredients in a heavy saucepan; heat over medium heat until sugar dissolves. Bring mixture to a boil; reduce heat and simmer for 30 minutes. Store, covered, in the refrigerator for up to one month. Makes 8 servings.

# Dips & Seasonings

## Must-Have Mustard

*Served over smoked ham…a new family tradition.*

1/4 c. coarse-grained mustard
1/4 c. Dijon mustard
1/4 c. dried basil

1/2 c. canola oil
3 T. brown sugar, packed
1/3 c. honey

Blend mustards and basil in a food processor until smooth; gradually blend in remaining ingredients. Cover and keep refrigerated. Makes 1-3/4 cups.

## Texas Tomato Salsa

*All the best of summertime…anytime.*

2  14-1/2 oz. cans stewed
    tomatoes
1/2 c. onion, finely chopped
juice of half a lime

1 t. salt
1/4 c. sliced green chilies
3 T. fresh cilantro, chopped
garlic salt and pepper to taste

Blend all the ingredients together in a food processor to desired smoothness. Makes 4 cups.

Toss in a few fresh
tomatoes from the garden
when giving away a jar of salsa
and don't forget
the recipe!

# Robust Spaghetti Sauce

*A guaranteed hearty meal.*

4-lb. bone-in pork roast
1/4 c. all-purpose flour
1/3 c. olive oil
2 c. hot water
4 cloves garlic, pressed
1 onion, chopped
2 bay leaves
1-1/2 t. celery salt
2 t. pepper
2 t. sugar

1/2 t. cayenne pepper
1/2 t. dried oregano
1/2 t. dried basil
1/8 t. nutmeg
4  6-oz. cans tomato paste
4 c. water
1 c. sliced mushrooms
1/2 c. sliced black olives
1 T. garlic salt

Coat pork roast in flour; brown in olive oil on all sides. Add hot water; cover and simmer until meat is tender, about 3 hours. Shred meat with 2 forks; add to large stockpot. Mix in remaining ingredients; stir until well combined. Cover and simmer for 2 hours, stirring occasionally; uncover and heat until desired consistency. Remove bay leaves before serving. Makes 3-1/2 quarts.

Make a meal! Place a jar of Robust Spaghetti Sauce in a new colander, add bread sticks and a box of pasta. Include a cookie mix for dessert...an extra-sweet surprise.

# Dips & Seasonings

## Sloppy Joe Mix

*Surprise coaches, teachers or scout leaders with this mix!*

2 T. dried, minced onion
2 T. dried green pepper flakes
1-1/2 t. salt
2 t. cornstarch

1/4 t. dry mustard
1 t. celery seed
1/2 t. chili powder
1/2 t. garlic salt

Mix ingredients together until well blended; store in an airtight container. Attach instructions. Makes about 5 tablespoons.

## Instructions:

Brown one pound ground beef in a skillet; drain. Add seasoning mix, 1/2 cup water and an 8-ounce can tomato sauce; bring to a boil. Reduce heat; simmer for 10 minutes, stirring often. Spoon onto buns to serve. Makes 6 servings.

Tuck a packet of Sloppy Joe Mix inside a
skillet...deliver to a newlywed couple.

## Easy Cheesy Pizza Dip

*Make it a supreme...add pepperoni, mushrooms and other toppings along with the peppers and onions.*

8-oz. pkg. cream cheese,
    softened
1 t. Italian seasoning
1/2 c. shredded
    Mozzarella cheese
1/4 c. plus 2 T. grated
    Parmesan cheese

8-oz. can pizza sauce
2 T. green pepper, chopped
2 T. onions, sliced
1 T. garlic salt

Combine cream cheese and Italian seasoning; mix well. Spread in the bottom of a 2-quart baking dish. Combine cheeses; sprinkle half cheese mixture over cream cheese. Spread pizza sauce over cheese. Top with remaining cheese, peppers, onions and garlic salt. Bake at 350 degrees for 15 to 18 minutes or until cheese is melted and mixture is bubbling around the edges. Serve with tortilla chips. Makes 6 to 8 servings.

Bring along a tasty appetizer to the next gathering! Place a container of Easy Cheesy Pizza Dip and some tortilla chips in a small pizza box and deliver to your hostess...they'll love it!

# Dips & Seasonings

## Creamy Red Pepper Dip

*Try this hearty treat on toasted pita too.*

7-1/2 oz. jar roasted red
    peppers, drained
4-oz. can chopped green chilies,
    drained
1 c. sour cream

1 c. mayonnaise
1 T. lemon juice
1/2 t. garlic powder
1/2 T. fresh cilantro, chopped

Mix ingredients until well blended; chill. Serve with vegetables or chips. Makes about 3 cups.

## Garlic & Bean Dip

*Spread on flour tortillas, roll up, chill and slice for a tasty appetizer!*

2 c. pinto beans, cooked
1/4 c. mayonnaise-type salad
    dressing
1 clove garlic, chopped

1-1/2 t. chili powder
1/4 t. salt
1/8 t. pepper

Combine all ingredients, mixing well. Cover and chill for one hour. Serve with tortilla chips. Makes about 2-1/2 cups.

*for you!*

# Ranch Dip & Dressing Mix

*A classic that never lasts long...the mix makes a great gift anytime!*

2 t. celery salt
2 t. garlic powder
3 T. dried, minced onion
2 t. pepper

2 t. sugar
2-1/2 t. paprika
2-1/2 t. dried parsley

Combine ingredients; blend well. Store in an airtight container. Attach instructions for dressing and mix. Makes 1/2 cup mix.

## Dip:

Blend one tablespoon mix with one cup sour cream. Refrigerate at least one hour before serving.

## Dressing:

Combine one tablespoon mix with one cup mayonnaise and one cup buttermilk. Makes 2 cups.

Give a garden in a can! Fill a vintage watering can with a variety of flower, vegetable and herb seeds...add some gloves, a few garden markers and a gardening magazine.

# Dips & Seasonings

## Easiest Cheese Ball

*Make 'em mini...just roll into 6 small balls,*
*wrap individually and give with some crackers.*

2 8-oz. pkgs. cream cheese
2 8-oz. pkgs. shredded sharp
   Cheddar cheese

1-oz. pkg. ranch dressing mix
1/4 t. hot pepper sauce
10-oz. pkg. chopped pecans

Combine cream cheese, Cheddar, dressing mix and hot pepper sauce; form into one large ball. Roll ball into chopped pecans to cover. Refrigerate overnight before serving. Makes 12 servings.

## Party Dill Dip Blend

*Include this seasoning mix with a round loaf of pumpernickel*
*for an instant party!*

1/2 c. dill weed
1/2 c. dried, minced onion
1/2 c. dried parsley
1/4 t. celery seed

1 T. paprika
1 T. garlic powder
1 T. dried thyme
2 t. celery salt

Combine ingredients; store in an airtight container. Attach instructions. Makes about 2 cups.

## Instructions:

Whisk 3 tablespoons mix with one cup mayonnaise and one cup sour cream. Refrigerate at least one to 2 hours before serving. Makes about 2-1/2 cups.

# Creamy Artichoke Spread

*Always a party pleaser...make some for your hostess!*

2 8-oz. pkgs. cream cheese
2 t. garlic, chopped
1-1/2 t. salt
14-oz. can artichoke hearts,
    drained and chopped
1/3 c. sliced black olives

7 green onions, chopped
6 T. sun-dried tomatoes,
    chopped
1/4 c. fresh parsley, chopped
1 t. fresh chives, chopped

Combine cream cheese, garlic and salt in a medium mixing bowl; stir in artichoke hearts and olives. Add remaining ingredients, mixing gently. Refrigerate overnight to blend flavors. Serves 6.

Line a small flowerpot with parchment paper and fill with Creamy Artichoke Spread. Place it in a larger flowerpot and fill the gap with ice cubes...it will stay cold when taking to a friend or neighbor.

# Dips & Seasonings

## Caesar Salad Dressing Mix

*They'll grow their own salad when you include romaine lettuce seed packets with this dressing mix.*

1 T. lemon zest
2/3 c. fresh Parmesan cheese, grated
1 T. dried oregano

1-1/2 t. dry mustard
1 t. pepper
1 t. garlic powder
1/2 t. cayenne pepper

Combine ingredients; store in an airtight container in the refrigerator for up to one month. Add instructions. Makes about one cup.

## Instructions:

Whisk together 1/3 cup vegetable oil, 1/4 cup Caesar Salad Dressing Mix, 3 tablespoons lemon juice, 2 tablespoons mayonnaise and one teaspoon anchovy paste. Toss with 12 cups romaine lettuce. Makes 6 to 8 servings.

Set a container of Caesar Salad Dressing Mix and salad tongs inside a wooden salad bowl...a clever bridal shower or wedding gift.

# Cranberry Vinegar with Fruit

*Add a few quartered orange slices for additional color!*

6 to 8 c. frozen cranberries          4 c. white vinegar
2/3 c. sugar

Tightly pack cranberries into a wide-mouth 6 to 8-cup clear jar; set
aside. Stir sugar into vinegar until dissolved; pour over fruit, covering
fruit. If necessary, blend one cup additional vinegar with 2 to
3 tablespoons sugar and add to fruit until it is completely covered.
Tightly cover jar so that it's airtight; set in a cool, dark place at least
2 weeks or up to 3 months, adding more vinegar-sugar solution to
keep fruit covered, if necessary. Keep refrigerated after opening. Makes
6 to 8 cups.

If fruit floats to the top
of the vinegar and is not
completely submerged, it
will discolor...place a
ball of plastic wrap over
the fruit and beneath
the lid to keep
it immersed.

Feel free
to copy these
and use
colored pens
to give
them some
Zing!

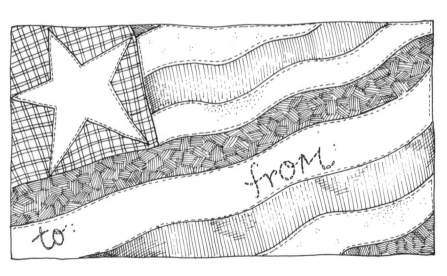

from.

to:

from our
home to
~yours~

Welcome!
from:

To:

From:

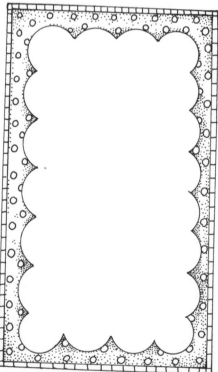

Make a whole jar of soap~

~just pour into ice cube trays.

Slip bath sachets into a new pair of fuzzy bath slippers...

Personalize a new dish and fill with pet treats!

Spotty.

Nifty Gifties

Personalize Your package by gluing a wooden letter to the box lid.

Include a good book when creating a bath basket.

Craft Glue

# Raspberry Bath Salts

*Pamper a friend with the scent of fresh raspberries.*

2 4-lb. cartons Epsom salts, divided
6 c. sea salt, divided
1/2 t. glycerin, divided

14 drops raspberry essential oil, divided
14 drops red food color
12 12-oz. jars and lids

Empty one carton Epsom salts into a large mixing bowl; add 3 cups sea salt, stirring well. Mix in 1/4 teaspoon glycerin and 7 drops oil; mix well and set aside. In a separate mixing bowl, combine remaining salts; stir well. Add remaining glycerin, oil and red food color; stir until completely blended and colored. Holding each jar at an angle, layer salts in jars, alternating white and colored mixtures. Seal lids and attach gift tags. Makes 12 jars.

Make a clever bath pillow to tuck in with some pampering goodies. Just sprinkle flower petals and fresh herbs on a towel, roll up and tie each end with wide ribbon. So easy!

# Nifty Gifties

## Piña Colada Tub Fizzy

*Slip these into the pocket of a new fuzzy robe.*

1 c. citric acid
1 c. baking soda
1 c. milk
1/2 t. pineapple essential oil
1/2 t. coconut essential oil

1 t. olive oil
10 drops yellow food coloring
witch hazel
2-oz. soap molds

Combine citric acid, baking soda and milk; blend very well. Stir in oils, olive oil and food coloring. Spritz witch hazel over mixture while stirring with the other hand. Once mixture begins to stick together, immediately pour into molds; let dry for 5 to 10 minutes and pop them out. Allow to air dry for 3 to 4 hours. Makes about fourteen, 2-ounce fizzies.

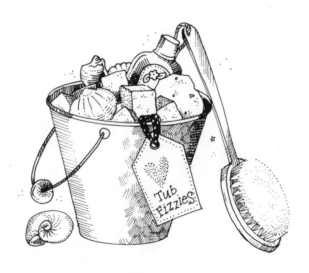

Need a last-minute housewarming gift? Fill a shower caddy with tub fizzies, a loofah, shower gel and body lotion...great for someone heading off to college too!

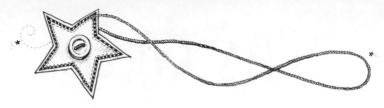

## Simply Citrus Lip Balm

*Luxurious and yummy!*

4 t. olive oil
1-1/2 t. beeswax, grated
1 t. shea butter
1 t. honey
3 drops lemon essential oil

3 drops orange essential oil
10 drops vitamin E oil
5 drops yellow food coloring
4  1/2-oz. lidded pots

In a double boiler, melt olive oil, beeswax, shea butter and honey together; remove from heat, allowing to cool for several minutes. Add essential and vitamin E oils. Set mixture aside until it firms up to shortening consistency. Stir in food coloring. Divide equally among pots and allow to cool. Makes 4 pots.

Have fun designing labels for lip balm...look at craft stores for round labels, colorful stickers and mini rubber stamps.

# Nifty Gifties

## Pepperminty Lip Balm

*Surprise guests with these as refreshing party favors!*

6 T. almond oil
2 t. honey
4 t. beeswax, grated

5 drops vitamin E oil
5 drops peppermint essential oil
8 1/2-oz. lidded pots

In a double boiler, melt almond oil, honey and beeswax together; remove from heat, allowing mixture to cool slightly. Add vitamin E and peppermint oils; stir until well blended. Pour into pots and allow to cool before covering. Makes 8 pots.

## Honey-Vanilla Lip Balm

*Have all your girlfriends over and make homemade lip balm together!*

1/2 c. almond oil
2 T. beeswax, grated
1 T. honey

1/2 t. vanilla essential oil
10 1/2-oz. lidded pots

In a double boiler, melt almond oil and beeswax. Remove from heat and immediately stir in honey and essential oil. Pour into pots; let cool before covering. Makes 10 pots.

Make an "All Grown Up" basket for a young lady! Include some sheer lip gloss, nail polish, a hand mirror, glittery body lotion and plenty of hair accessories.

## Silky-Smooth Body Powder

*Tie on an oversized make-up brush with a pretty ribbon.*

2 c. cornstarch
1 c. tapioca flour

2 T. cocoa butter, finely grated
3/4 t. essential oil

Combine all ingredients in a large jar; shake well. Divide into pretty pots and attach gift tags. Makes about 3 cups.

## Orange-Coconut Creamy Lotion

*A dried orange slice tied with a length of raffia makes a fragrant tag.*

1/2 t. citric acid
4 T. coconut oil
4 to 5 drops orange essential oil

1 c. less 2 T. water
2 4-oz. bottles

Combine all ingredients in a microwave-safe container; microwave until just melted. Whisk quickly until mixture turns white and milky. Makes 2 bottles.

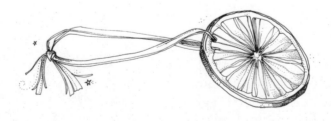

Pair some luxurious body powder with a bottle of
Orange-Coconut Creamy Lotion in an old-fashioned
milk carrier...charming!

# Nifty Gifties

## Strawberries & Cream Milk Bath Mix

*Moms, sisters, roommates…they'll all ask for more!*

1 c. powdered milk
3/4 c. sea salt

1/4 t. strawberry essential oil

Place milk and salt in a large bowl; mix well. Scoop out about 1/2 cup and place in a small bowl. Sprinkle oil over top of mix; stir well. Add oil mix back to large bowl; mix well. Store in an airtight jar. Attach a gift tag with instructions.

## Instructions:

Scoop out 1/4 cup and dissolve under running bath water.

Clever giftwrap makes a good gift better! Try the funny pages, maps, fabric, blankets and quilts, t-shirts, brown paper bags or even wallpaper.

# Gingerbread Mini Cookies & Giftbox

*Fill with hard candy and small toys too!*

| | |
|---|---|
| 1 c. shortening | 1 t. baking soda |
| 1 c. sugar | 1-1/4 t. salt |
| 1 c. molasses | 1 t. nutmeg |
| 5 c. all-purpose flour | 1 T. ground ginger |

Melt shortening in a large saucepan; mix in sugar and molasses. Combine remaining ingredients in a mixing bowl; gradually add to molasses mixture to form a stiff dough. Divide dough in two equal parts. On a floured surface, roll one part dough to 1/4-inch thickness; cut into twelve, 4-inch squares and place on ungreased baking sheets. Roll second part dough to 1/4-inch thickness; cut with mini cookie cutters and place on ungreased baking sheets. Bake cookies at 375 degrees for 13 to 15 minutes; let cool for several minutes on the baking sheet, then remove to wire rack. When cooled, place one square on a flat surface; use cement icing to attach four sides. Fill box with half the mini cookies and secure a lid with icing. Repeat with remaining squares and cookies. Makes 2 boxes filled with cookies.

## Decorator Icing:

| | |
|---|---|
| 2-1/2 c. powdered sugar | 2 egg whites |
| 1/4 t. cream of tartar | 1/2 t. vanilla extract |

In a medium bowl, combine sugar and cream of tartar; add egg white and vanilla. Beat until icing holds its shape. Add more sugar to thicken, if necessary.

# Nifty Gifties

## Cinnamon-Apple Ornaments

*These can also be painted with acrylic paint and sprayed with a matte spray sealer to protect them once they're dry.*

1 c. cinnamon
1 T. ground cloves
1 T. nutmeg

3/4 c. applesauce
2 T. craft glue

In a medium mixing bowl, combine cinnamon, cloves and nutmeg; mix in applesauce and glue. Knead mixture for 2 to 3 minutes to form a ball. Roll dough to 1/4-inch thickness; cut with cookie cutters. Use a toothpick to make a hole for hanging. Let air dry for 4 to 5 days, turning occasionally. Makes 4 to 5 dozen.

For a pretty stained-glass ornament, use a mini cookie cutter to cut out a "window" in each cinnamon-apple ornament. Fill with crushed hard candy and bake at 300 degrees for 10 minutes or until candy is melted.

# Heavenly Bubble Bath Soap

*Be an angel...perk up a friend with pampering bath soap.*

1/2 c. unscented hair shampoo
1/2 c. water

5-1/2 t. baby oil
1/2 t. vanilla essential oil

Combine all ingredients in a container with a lid; secure lid and shake. Attach instructions for gift giving. Makes 1-1/2 cups.

## Instructions:

Add 2 to 3 tablespoons to warm bath water. Contains enough for about 8 heavenly bubble baths.

Bubble Bath Day is January 8th! Celebrate by giving your girlfriends Heavenly Bubble Bath Soap, a yummy-smelling candle and a fun magazine to read while relaxing.

# Nifty Gifties

## Herbal Oatmeal Bath Sachet

*These single-use sachets are great for weddings, showers
or anytime...just toss 'em under running water!*

1 c. long-cooking oats,
   uncooked
1/2 c. dried or fresh lavender

1/2 c. dried or fresh rose petals
6-inch muslin square
washable ribbon

Combine oats, lavender and rose petals. Place 2 to 3 tablespoons
mixture in the center of muslin; bring the 4 corners together and tie in
the middle with a ribbon, making sure mixture is secure. Repeat with
remaining mixture. Makes about 16 sachets.

## Pampering Body Powder

*A silky-smooth finishing touch to a bath basket.*

1 c. cornstarch
1/2 c. baking soda

8 drops rose essential oil

Combine cornstarch and baking soda; add rose drops. Store in an
airtight container. Makes 1-1/2 cups.

Add a personal
touch by
stitching on a
monogram to
pillows, sachets, placemats
and napkins before giving.

## Natural Orange-Clove Candles

*New neighbor moving in? The scent of this gift can't be beat!*

tea light candle
orange
pen

paring knife
sand
whole cloves

Use tea light to trace circle on top of orange. Use paring knife to cut away circle, making sure tea light will fit snugly inside. Scoop out all orange pulp; refill with sand, leaving room for candle to sit flush with the top of the orange. Set tea light inside; line rim of opening with whole cloves.

## Garden Herb Candle

*Fresh herbs are pretty for a springtime gift too!*

old white candles
1 c. dried herbs

6" tall white pillar candle

Melt old candles in a double boiler. Spread ground herbs onto a baking sheet placed close to double boiler. Holding the wick of the pillar candle, dip into the melted wax; quickly roll it in herbs. Dip the candle again into the melted wax just enough to cover the herbs. Set on wax paper to harden.

Need a quick & easy gift? Wrap a sheer ribbon around a simple glass votive holder to cast a colorful glow...try red, pink and orange ribbons.

## Pressed Flower Candle

*Set in a basket with a fresh bouquet.*

6 c. water
6" tall white pillar candle
pressed flower petals

pressed leaves
1/4 bar paraffin wax

Bring water to a boil and remove from heat. Working quickly, hold candle by the wick and immerse in the hot water for 45 seconds. Immediately press a few flower petals and leaves onto the softened wax around the candle. Place paraffin in a small microwave-safe bowl; microwave for 3 to 4 minutes until melted. Using a small paintbrush, coat the flowers with a thin layer of paraffin.

Pressed flowers are easy to make at home...just sandwich blooms between tissue paper and cardboard. Set a heavy book and a brick on top and wait about 2 weeks. Perfect for crafts and decorating!

## Basic Melt & Pour Soap

*Look for glittery and pearlescent soap colorant...so pretty!*

soap mold
non-stick vegetable spray

4 oz. clear glycerin soap, grated
4 drops soap fragrance oil

Lightly coat soap mold with non-stick vegetable spray; wipe dry. Place glycerin in a microwave-safe measuring cup; heat on high for 15 seconds. Stir and heat in 5-second intervals until completely melted, making sure not to boil. Add fragrance, one drop at a time, mixing after each addition. When soap forms a skin in the measuring cup, move skin aside and pour soap into prepared mold. Cool completely before unmolding. Allow soap to cure 3 to 4 weeks before wrapping with clear plastic wrap. Makes one, 4-ounce bar.

Make a bath mitten! Fold a washcloth in half; sew 2 of the sides closed, leaving one side open. Sew on a loop and place a bar of soap inside.

# Nifty Gifties

## Festive Wrapped Soap

*Tie up in a fluffy new face cloth.*

soap bars
kraft paper
tape
old-fashioned giftwrap

scissors
sheer ribbon
matches
gold sealing wax with stamp

Neatly wrap each soap bar in kraft paper; tape to seal. Cut gift wrap into strips; wrap a strip around each bar, leaving the brown paper at the ends exposed; tape to seal. Cut ribbon into lengths long enough to wrap around each bar, securing each with a knot. Light the sealing wax stick and allow it to drip on top of the ribbon knot; press the stamp down for a few seconds to make the seal.

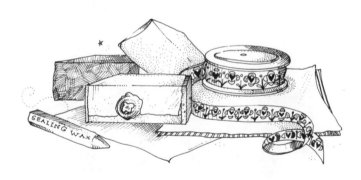

Dried rose buds, delicate ribbon and handmade paper add a touch of elegance when wrapping bars of soap.

# Victorian Rosemary Pomander

*This fragrant gift looks so pretty hung on a doorknob.*

2  16-inch lengths satin ribbon
4-inch floral foam ball
12 pearl-topped straight pins

30 sprigs fresh rosemary
floral scissors

Wrap ribbon around center of ball, inserting a pin to secure about every 2 inches. Wrap second ribbon around the center also making a cross at the top and bottom and dividing the sphere into four sections. Firmly push sprigs into each section, spacing them as evenly as possible. Gently clip sprigs to a uniform height as you work. When all sections are completely covered, trim to an even height. Gather excess ribbon together forming a loop from which to hang pomander.

Charming! Turn a gift box into a keepsake by using satin ribbons to cover the sides and bottom. Use a basket-weave pattern with several ribbons to cover the lid.

# Nifty Gifties

## Beaded Flowerpot Candle

*Have fun mixing & matching buttons, beads and paint colors!*

blue acrylic paint
4-inch terra cotta pot
hot glue
pearl beads

pillar candle
block of floral foam, cut into
    small cubes
small blue and pearl buttons

Paint flowerpot with blue paint, allow to dry. Apply a second coat if necessary. Hot glue pearl beads around pot rim to decorate; allow to dry completely. Place a pillar candle in the center of pot. Pack foam cubes around candle to secure. Hot glue buttons around candle base to completely cover foam.

Tie a gift tag on a Beaded Flowerpot Candle and write
"To a jewel of a friend."

# Old-Fashioned Lilac Perfume

*Look for vintage perfume lockets at flea markets and antique shops.*

1/4 c. beeswax, grated
1/4 c. petroleum jelly

1-1/2 t. lilac essential oil
12  1/2-oz. lidded tins

Melt beeswax and petroleum jelly together in a double boiler. Remove from heat, cool slightly and stir in essential oil. Pour into small tins and let air dry until firm. Makes 12 tins.

# Refreshing Face Splash

*Little cork-topped bottles are just right for holding this splash.*

3/4 c. rose water

2 T. witch hazel

Combine ingredients and store in a lidded bottle. Attach a gift tag with instructions. Makes about one cup.

## Instructions:

Splash a small handful on your face after cleansing.

A charm bracelet is a wonderful birthday or Mothers' Day gift. Give a new charm every year...look for charms that will remind her of special events or shared moments.

# Nifty Gifties

## Fresh-Scented Drawer Liners

*Easy as can be and so thoughtful!*

giftwrap
scented body spray
rubber band

plastic bag
satin ribbon

Cut wrapping paper into six, 24"x18" sheets. Spray the unprinted side of each sheet with body spray; allow to dry for 30 minutes. Roll sheets together tightly and secure with a rubber band. Slide roll into a plastic bag, tie closed and allow to sit overnight. Remove plastic bag and replace rubber band with satin ribbon before giving.

A year 'round gift! Renew a subscription to a friend's favorite magazine and bring joy each month...and there's no worry about color, style or fit!

## Polka Dot Button Frame

*Kids love to help with this crafty frame.*

acrylic paints
5" x 6" wooden craft frame
craft glue

several lengths of ribbon
assorted buttons

Paint frame in desired color; allow to dry. Glue ribbon onto frame forming an inside or outside border or in any desired design. Arrange buttons on entire frame before gluing and then glue buttons on one at a time and let dry.

## Rosebud Flower Frame

*Try lavender or rose petals...dried or fresh!*

cream acrylic paint
5" x 6" wooden craft frame
small, dried rosebuds

hot glue
other small, dried flowers

Paint frame; allow to dry. Hot glue rosebuds to frame, covering as much surface as possible. Fill in any open space with smaller flowers, gluing to secure.

Disguise a gift certificate or sporting event tickets, by placing them in a frame before giving...concert tickets fit great in a CD case too!

# Nifty Gifties

## Scented Personal Stationery

*Refresh the scent with just a few drops of scented oil.*

box of stationery
corrugated cardboard

10 drops honeysuckle
essential oil
cotton fabric

Remove stationery from box; cut cardboard to fit the bottom of the box. Pour honeysuckle drops on ridged side of cardboard; wrap cardboard in fabric. Place wrapped cardboard in the bottom of the box; replace stationery in box and close. Keep the box closed for one week before giving.

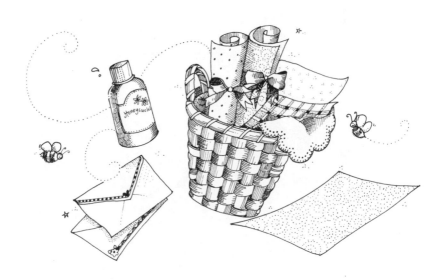

Homemade from the heart! Photocopy photos onto iron-on transfer paper available at craft and office supply stores. Iron onto crisp white fabric, frame with a ribbon border and sew into a pillow. It's "sew" easy!

# Lemon-Fresh Laundry Rinse

*Try lavender essential oil for spring-fresh laundry too!*

1 t. lemon essential oil                 1-qt. bottle white vinegar

Add oil to bottle of vinegar; secure lid and shake well. Attach instructions for giving. Makes one quart.

## Instructions:

Shake well before using. Measure 1/4 cup rinse and add to your laundry's final rinse in place of fabric softener. Contains enough for 16 lemon-fresh loads.

What a thoughtful housewarming or wedding gift. Fill a laundry basket with fluffy new towels and tuck in a bottle of Lemon-Fresh Laundry Rinse...don't forget the instructions!

# Nifty Gifties

## Lavender Drawer Sachet

*Make personalized sachets by rubber-stamping or embroidering an initial.*

2 5-inch squares decorative
    fabric
dried lavender

2 to 3 drops lavender
    essential oil
Optional: charms and
    ribbon roses

Place right sides of fabric squares together and sew, leaving bottom open for turning and filling. In a small bowl, crush lavender with bottom of a drinking glass; add oil and toss to mix. Turn sachet so right side is out; fill with lavender mix and stitch closed. Decorate with charms and ribbon roses, if desired.

Make several heart-shaped sachets using shimmery fabrics to give as bridesmaids' gifts...or tie one on a bridal shower gift.

## Meow Munchies

*Lavish your furry friends with these extra-special treats.*

1 c. canned tuna, drained
1-1/2 c. whole-grain bread
    crumbs
1/2 t. brewers' yeast

1-1/2 T. oil
1 egg, beaten
1 t. garlic powder

In a medium bowl, use a fork to separate tuna into tiny pieces; mix in remaining ingredients. Drop by 1/4 teaspoonfuls onto greased baking sheets. Bake at 350 degrees for 8 minutes. Cool to room temperature and refrigerate. Makes 4 cups.

## Catnip Cut-Out Cookies

*Kitties go crazy over these cookies.*

1 c. whole-wheat flour
1/4 c. soy flour
1 t. catnip
1/3 c. powdered milk
2 T. wheat germ

1 t. garlic powder
1/3 c. milk
1 T. molasses
1 egg
2 T. butter, melted

Combine first 6 ingredients in a mixing bowl; stir in milk, molasses, egg and butter. Roll dough to 1/4-inch thickness on a well-greased baking sheet; cut into small pieces. Bake at 350 degrees for 20 minutes; let cool and store in an airtight container. Makes 5 to 6 dozen pieces.

# Nifty Gifties

## Bone Appetit Dog Biscuits

*Pair with a collar for a new puppy!*

3 c. all-purpose flour
3 c. whole-wheat flour
2 c. cracked wheat
1 c. cornmeal
2-1/2 t. garlic powder

1 T. brewers' yeast
1/2 c. powdered milk
3 c. beef broth, divided
2 T. milk

Combine first 7 ingredients in a large bowl. Stir in 2 cups broth to form a very stiff dough; gradually mix in remaining cup broth to form bread-dough consistency. On a floured surface, roll dough to 1/4-inch thickness. Use cookie cutters to cut dough into shapes; place biscuits on greased baking sheets. Lightly brush tops with milk. Bake at 300 degrees for 45 minutes; turn oven off without removing biscuits. Allow biscuits to sit overnight. Store in an airtight container. Makes 4-1/2 pounds.

Pamper pets with a personalized dish filled with treats.
Write their name on it and wrap it up in colored
cellophane...tie on a toy and they'll love it!

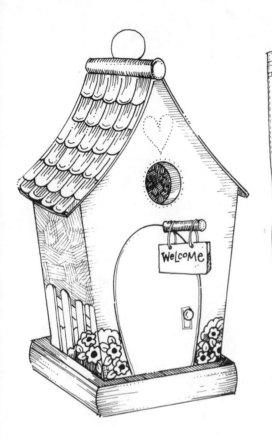

Especially
for YOU from

Hey! You can
# use our
# labels
on your goodies!
Just take 'em to
your copy machine
& run some copies.

★ Cut 'em out,
color 'em with
markers & tie 'em on.

Homemade!

MMMMMM ♥ GOOD! ♥
If · I · Do · Say · So · Myself

# Index

# Index

## Dips & Seasonings

## Muffins & Breads

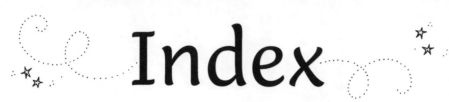

# Index

# We've cooked up a whole collection of Gooseberry Patch® books!

Have a taste for more? Call us toll-free at

## 1-800-854-6673

We'll send you our latest catalog filled with snowmen, Santas, ornaments, candles, cookie cutters, gourmet goodies, calendars, giftwrap, pottery, collectibles and MORE...including our best-selling cookbooks!

**Phone us:**
1·800·854·6673

**Fax us:**
1·740·363·7225

**Visit our website:**
gooseberrypatch.com

# Send us your favorite recipe!

*Include the memory that makes it special for you too!*\* If we select your recipe for a brand new **Gooseberry Patch** cookbook, your name will appear right along with it...and you'll receive a FREE copy of the book! Mail to:

Vickie & Jo Ann
**Gooseberry Patch**, Dept. Book
600 London Road
Delaware, Ohio 43015

\*Please include the number of servings and all other necessary information!

quick as a wink ⏱ make memories ♥ surprise a friend ☆! get crafty ✎ vintage jars 🎁 homespun squares baked with love from me to you! mix it up ♥ tied up with a bow pretty paper gift tags yummy gifts vintage photos cheer!